TREMBLE

Blind Faith? or Just Blind?

DAVE FIEDLER

Remnant
Publications
Coldwater MI 49036

TREMBLE
Blind Faith? or Just Blind?
by Dave Fiedler

Also by the author—
Hindsight: Seventh-day Adventist History in Essays and Extracts
d'Sozo: Reversing the Worst Evil

Copyright © 2014 by
Remnant Publications, Inc.
All Rights Reserved
Printed in the United States of America

Cover design by David Berthiaume
Text Design by Greg Solie • Altamont Graphics

ISBN: 978-1-62913-044-6

Contents

Introduction

THERE are, unfortunately, few things as potentially divisive as theology. And since this book deals with theology, it runs that risk. That's a shame, because the real focus needs to be saving souls—protecting them from dangerous error in the first place, and reclaiming those who have already accepted or even advocated those errors.

I fear that focus may be lost by many who read these pages. To some degree, that will be the fault of the author. I struggle to achieve and maintain the right balance and perspective, but I have more than enough pride of opinion and general purpose obstinacy to get me in trouble. For my failings in this, I apologize. I wish I had all the wisdom and tact of Jesus.

What scares me in this regard is the story of John Harvey Kellogg. Because that story is full of lessons, I wrote on it at some length in my last book, and I felt compelled to recap the story as the basis from which to understand the challenges addressed by this book. What makes it important? Among other things, we lost a great deal when we lost Dr. Kellogg. Ellen White once referred to him as "the greatest physician in our world, a man to whom the Lord has given understanding and knowledge." [1]

That was the blessing God had given the church in Dr. Kellogg. But by 1907, when he was formally disfellowshiped, Kellogg had become a great danger to the church. Yet history and inspiration both lay at least some of the fault for that change at the feet of his brethren.

I have no doubt that they meant well. They sought to protect the church's doctrinal purity, and that was good. But at times, in their humanity—the same kind of humanity you and I possess today—they made serious mistakes. They sometimes lacked the wisdom and tact of Jesus.

---

1   *Manuscript Releases*, vol. 5, 406

There's another thing that scares me in all this, too. That is my lack of skill in separating co-mingled elements of good and evil. I don't always recognize good when I see it, and sometimes evil doesn't register as clearly as I wish it would. Even worse, I sometimes suffer from a spiritual dyslexia in which I call evil good, and good evil. Isaiah rightly labeled such failings a source of "woe." [2] That I may be tested in this way is a solemn and, frankly, frightening thought. Others have been given warnings which surely apply similarly to me—and the stakes are high.

In 1885 there was a revival in the Healdsburg, California, church. It was flawed; some fanaticism developed, and so the most prominent ministers in the vicinity, men whom we rightly respect for their contributions to the Lord's work, simply shut it down. Ellen White's response is sobering:

> I wish to say some things in reference to the revival at Healdsburg.
>
> I wish to say I am not in harmony with your treatment of this matter. That there were fanatical ones who pressed into that work I would not deny. But if you move in the future as you have done in this matter, you may be assured of one thing, you will condemn the work of the latter rain when it shall come. For you will see at that time far greater evidences of fanaticism. ...
>
> I cannot sanction your course. I cannot see that while you were working to correct evils, as you might have done, that you should stop the work. If this is the way you manage when God sends good, be assured the revivals will be rare. When the Spirit of God comes it will be called fanaticism, as on the day of Pentecost. [3]

Such a warning raises concerns in my mind, both for myself and for many of my more conservative brethren. I fear the best of us have ample cause to pray for mercy and grace, lest we face such a test unprepared.

---

2   Isaiah 5:20

3   *Manuscript Releases*, vol. 21, 147. For more information on this circumstance, see *Charismatic Experiences In Early Seventh-day Adventist History*, 28–30

And so it is with some misgivings that I put forth my thoughts and findings on this subject. I wish there were no need to. But I have found much that causes concern. Ideas are being spread abroad that, I believe, pose a serious danger to souls for whom Christ died. It is time for us to carefully weigh the matter. We're back where we were, once before.

> If ever there was a time when the writings of every one connected with our work should be closely criticized, it is now. The Lord has made known to me that His word is to be studied, and as no such representations as those made in *Living Temple* are made in the word, we are to reject them. We are to take the word as God has given it to us. If Christ had thought it essential for such theories to be presented to human minds, He would have included them in His teachings. As our Owner and Redeemer, He has put in His word all the instruction that is necessary for our salvation. [4]

And so, however successfully or imperfectly this volume manages the task, the double challenge is still there: we must remain faithful to the truth as revealed in Scripture, and we must embrace the mission of One who was willing to die to save sinners. May God help us each.

Dave Fiedler
July 2014

---

4   *Counsels to Writers and Editors*, 158

Chapter One
Way Back Then

IN the late 1890s and early 1900s, the Seventh-day Adventist Church faced one of its greater challenges in the apostasy of Dr. John Harvey Kellogg. We commonly speak of the doctor's "pantheism" as *the* issue which threatened the church and resulted in his loss of membership. This is simply inaccurate, and that's why the idea survives: it's simple. But it certainly wasn't the prevailing view at the time.

There had been conflict between Kellogg and the Adventist ministry in general—and a number of prominent church administrators in specific—since the 1880s, and especially so since the mid 1890s.[5] Pantheism didn't become "an issue" until after the Battle Creek Sanitarium burned down on February 18, 1902, and Kellogg's book, *The Living Temple*, was offered as a fund-raising mechanism to assist the rebuilding effort. Then the book's clearly pantheistic (technically, pan*en*theistic) content raised concerns. The General Conference Executive Committee appointed a sub-committee of four to examine its teachings: three found no fault, one branded it heresy.

Eventually, the sole dissenter (W.W. Prescott) carried the majority of the General Conference's decision makers with him, and it was voted that the church would not publish or endorse the book. Dr. Kellogg seems to have considered this an isolated over-reaction, and made arrangements for the Review and Herald Publishing Association to print the book as a private contract.

On the night of December 30, 1902, the printing plates for *The Living Temple* were on the press-room floor, ready to go on the presses. And they would have, if the Review had not burned to the ground that night.

But "pantheism" was not only a late-comer to the list of conflicts, it was seen as a muddy enough issue that many paid it little attention. There were, after all, much more long-standing differences which

---

5   For a fascinating look at the "Kellogg crisis" and its effect on the church, see *d'Sozo: Reversing the Worst Evil*, available from Remnant Publications.

arose from financial matters related to Kellogg's desire to expand the medical work, and a more general conflict fueled by the doctor's resistance to what he saw as the General Conference's efforts to take control of what he considered *his* domain.

The sanitarium had only been partially insured at the time of the fire, and Kellogg faced a major task in raising funds for its rebuilding. Aside from the plan to sell books, one method he turned to was the sale of bonds. Likely he hoped to eventually persuade the bond holders to make the money an outright contribution, but in the meantime he would do what he needed to do to get cash.

As it became apparent that Kellogg's construction plans went far beyond anything anyone else had expected—and far afield from the instruction given over the years by Ellen White—the bonds themselves became an issue. At the General Conference of 1903, Ellen White spoke against the bonds, saying it was not God's will that the funds of church members should be so largely tied up in the sanitarium at a time when openings for mission work were appearing all around the world.[6]

This may sound like Ellen White was *against* Dr. Kellogg. Wrong. She was against the errors on both sides of this argument that dishonored the Lord. There was much to be said in favor of Dr. Kellogg, as she had demonstrated just the day before:

> After the meeting at Minneapolis, Dr. Kellogg was a converted man, and we all knew it. We could see the converting power of God working in his heart and life. …
>
> Many souls have been converted; many wonderful cures have been wrought. The Lord stood by the side of Dr. Kellogg as he performed difficult operations. When the doctor was overwrought by taxing labor, God understood the situation, and He put His hand on Dr. Kellogg's hand as he operated, and through His power the operations were successful.
>
> I wish this to be understood. Over and over again I have encouraged Dr. Kellogg, telling him that the Lord God of Israel was at his right hand, to help him, and to give him success as he

---

6   *General Conference Bulletin*, April 7, 1903

performed the difficult operations that meant life or death to the ones operated upon. I told the doctor that before he took up his instruments to operate upon patients, he must pray for them. The patients saw that Dr. Kellogg was under the jurisdiction of God, that he understood His power to carry on the work successfully, and they had more confidence in him than in worldly physicians.

God has given Dr. Kellogg the success that he has had. I have tried constantly to keep this before him, telling him that it was God who was working with him, and that the truth of God was to be magnified by His physician. God will bless every other physician who will yield himself wholly to God, and will be with his hand when he works.

This was the light given. God worked that the medical missionary work might stand on the highest vantage ground; that it might be known that Seventh-day Adventists have a God working with them, a God who has a constant oversight of His work.

God does not endorse the efforts put forth by different ones to make the work of Dr. Kellogg as hard as possible, in order to build themselves up. God gave the light on health reform, and those who rejected it rejected God. One and another who knew better said that it all came from Dr. Kellogg, and they made war upon him. This had a bad influence on the doctor. He put on the coat of irritation and retaliation. God did not want him to stand in the position of warfare, and He does not want you to stand there.

Those who have turned away from the Battle Creek Sanitarium to get worldly physicians to care for them did not realize what they were doing. God established the Battle Creek Sanitarium. God worked through Dr. Kellogg; but men did not realize this. When they were sick, they sent for worldly physicians to come, because of something that the doctor had said or done that did not please them. This God did not approve.[7]

---

7   *General Conference Bulletin*, April 6, 1903

Bear in mind that these comments were made in a public meeting, to an audience largely composed of ministers, at a General Conference session. Indeed, Ellen White could speak rather directly when circumstances called for it!

And remember as well, that this was the spring of 1903. A year after the *Living Temple* debate had begun, one would not be incorrect in saying that the prophet of the Lord was, to some degree at least, defending a pantheist!

But note this carefully: She *wasn't* defending pantheism! In fact, you can search the entire *General Conference Bulletin* from 1903—not just Ellen White's talks, but every word recorded from every speaker—and you will not find "pantheism" or "pantheist" a single time. That simply wasn't the issue of the moment. Does that mean it was a *non-issue*? Of course not; just not the issue of the moment.

Another doctor—a close friend of almost everyone on both sides of the conflict, one who knew Kellogg well for many years both before and after the crisis, and an active participant in many of the key events—has left us an account of the issues. His name was Sanford Edwards, and he described it this way:

> Kellogg was desperately pressed from two sides. He needed the denominational influence to supply money to buy bonds to pay for his new building. The bonds were a drug on the market without denominational approval, and Sister White condemned them. That hurt Kellogg awfully. The medical school was deteriorating for lack of students as were his nursing classes. Kellogg was ready to surrender along theological lines, but not on control. It was on the control that he had his backing. Jones, Magan, Sutherland, and others I could name, some conference officers and some ministers, feared centralization of power. That was the real issue all along. Other things like personalities and points of difference on theological points were incidental and gave points to talk about, but the issue was the centralization of power in the General Conference committee. [8]

Among other things, Kellogg had opened himself up for criticism by replacing the already-too-large sanitarium with a building

---

8   Sanford P.S. Edwards, *Memoirs of SDA Pioneers,* 33

nearly twice the size. Ellen White had often said it would be better for the working force of the sanitarium to be spread out over separate and scattered smaller institutions. But Kellogg knew that he could retain more influence in one locality than he could in ten, so he ignored her counsel and went for broke. He tried to deflect criticism on this point by saying:

> In making our plans, we made them not quite so large as before in regard to the accommodation of patients. … in the buildings that were burned there were 341 rooms for patients. In our new building we have 296 rooms for patients.

Never mind that the patient rooms (and everything else about the new building) were larger and more luxurious than before.

Aware that this portrayal of "down sizing" alone might not be persuasive, the doctor deftly appeared to be as cooperative as could be while dropping a rather significant threat of disrupting the lives of thousands of Adventists in and around Battle Creek:

> Now if we have made a mistake in erecting this building, the mistake can be corrected. The building can be sold, the entire institution can be sold. There are parties who will be very glad to buy. I know parties who would be glad to purchase it. … If it is best that this enterprise should be abandoned at Battle Creek, then this property can be sold. There is no difficulty about it; and if this Conference will take action to that effect, that the Battle Creek Sanitarium should be sold, that it was a mistake that it should be erected there, and it should be sold, I will guarantee that it can be sold in a very short time, and on such terms as will leave the corporation in a better state financially than it would have been after the fire if we had abandoned the enterprise as it was. … If this Conference will vote that this enterprise shall be abandoned at Battle Creek, the property can be sold promptly, and the enterprise there can be off your hands. [9]

Note that it was "the corporation" that would be better off financially, not "the denomination."

---

9   *General Conference Bulletin*, April 6, 1903, 83

Things like this, dozens of times over, were making the working relationship between Dr. Kellogg and the officers of the General Conference very strained. And notice, Kellogg wasn't the only one at fault. Those people who had tried to make "the work of Dr. Kellogg as hard as possible, in order to build themselves up," included ministers and administrators of the church.

And, too, it should be noted that the single most divisive and disputed action taken at that 1903 General Conference session was the rewriting of the denomination's barely two-year-old constitution so as to bring all institutions of the church (wishful thinking included the sanitarium) under the ownership of the various conferences—exactly what Kellogg had feared for years.

Truth be told, this whole conflict was the unhappy result of fairly normal levels of pride and stubbornness on both sides of the divide. If we had to put a name on the result, it would probably be "politics"—two groups, each pressing for the outcome that seemed best to them. A century and more later, we may debate the wisdom and even wonder about the sincerity of those involved, but the record is clear that each side was certainly human enough to occasionally say and do things that were deserving of the Lord's correction.

Now, don't assume that both groups were equally right, or equally wrong, or equally righteous, or equally anything. With human beings involved, it's a fair bet to say that there was *some* good and *some* bad in all. The most amazing aspect of the story is the role played by the elderly woman who refused to side fully with either party, but solidly stood her ground in the middle, continually calling all involved to restore unity on a basis of truth.

Unfortunately, her efforts at the 1903 General Conference failed. One of the least helpful events to follow was Dr. Kellogg's printing of three thousand copies of *The Living Temple*—this time at a non-Adventist press. Ellen White received a copy in due course, but chose not to read any of it until September 23. Then she saw with her natural sight the things of which the Lord had been warning her for some time.

The next opportunity to work this all out with the people involved came in early October when the General Conference held its first Autumn Council at the new headquarters in Takoma Park. After the conflicts of the General Conference session some months before, every church administrator from the president on down was hoping for a calm, unifying, productive opportunity to get some "real" work done. It was not to be.

> The Autumn Council of the General Conference Committee opened in Washington, D.C., according to plan on October 7. … In the early days of the Council, Dr. E.J. Waggoner, Elder A.T. Jones, and Dr. David Paulson arrived in Washington. Dr. Kellogg came Sabbath morning, October 17. As the men from Battle Creek presented themselves, it was evident to Elder Daniells and his associates that they would again be confronted with *The Living Temple* and the teaching of pantheism."[10]

This time, pantheism *was* the issue of the moment. Kellogg and his associates pressed the Council to reconsider *The Living Temple* and the "new philosophy" it contained. Some of these men actually seem to have believed there was great value in the teachings Kellogg had set forth (Paulson, for instance), while others were likely just as motivated by more political concerns. Whatever their motivation, it would be hard to question the commitment of men willing to place their careers on the line in defense of positions that were clearly unpopular with the highest administrators of the organization which wrote their paychecks.

The debate filled one full day, ending in an acrimonious stalemate. Daniells, in the role of chairman, simply dismissed the meeting that night without a vote. Contention, confusion, and complexity made it foolish to press for any resolution.

> Dr. Paulson, who was strongly supportive of Dr. Kellogg, joined Daniells [on his way home after the meeting]. As the two walked along they continued with the discussion of the day. Reaching the home where Daniells was staying, they stood under a lamppost and chatted for a time. Finally, Dr. Paulson shook his finger at Daniells and declared:

---

10   *Ellen G. White: The Early Elmshaven Years*, 296

"You are making the mistake of your life. After all this turmoil, some of these days you will wake up to find yourself rolled in the dust, and another will be leading the forces."[11]

Daniells, probably slightly shaken, walked up the steps to the boarding house, opened the door, and went inside. There, the atmosphere was decidedly more joyous. In his memoir, written thirty-three years after the event, Daniells recalls being greeted with the exclamation, "Deliverance has come! Here are two messages from Mrs. White."[12]

These messages, prompted by the famous "Iceberg Vision" (and written in California some time before they were mailed so as to arrive in Takoma Park at just the right time) were unequivocal: pantheism—and anything akin to it—was not to be accepted as a part of the third angel's message. It was in this context that Ellen White employed the memorable term "Alpha" to describe Kellogg's teachings.

> I was instructed that certain sentiments in *Living Temple* were the Alpha of a long list of deceptive theories.[13]

"Alpha," of course, is the first letter of the Greek alphabet. That is significant because of Ellen White's follow-on comments in which she employed the imagery of the last letter of the Greek alphabet, the "omega":

> Be not deceived; many will depart from the faith, giving heed to seducing spirits and doctrines of devils. We have now before us the Alpha of this danger. The Omega will be of a most startling nature.[14]

> In the book *Living Temple* there is presented the Alpha of deadly heresies. The Omega will follow, and will be received

---

11   *Ellen G. White: The Early Elmshaven Years*, 296–297

12   *The Abiding Gift of Prophecy*, 337

13   *Sermons and Talks*, vol. 1, 343

14   *Selected Messages*, Book One, 197. Ellen White did not always capitalize the terms "Alpha" and "Omega" when she used them in this context. We have chosen to consistently capitalize these words when they apply to the two apostasies, the one in Kellogg's day, and the other at the end of time.

by those who are not willing to heed the warning God has given. [15]

Living Temple contains the Alpha of these theories. I knew that the Omega would follow in a little while; and I trembled for our people.[16]

There is little said directly about the "Omega," but those three comments are enough to capture the attention of anyone interested in the future of God's church. So what's the "Omega of deadly heresies" going to be? We aren't told, exactly. But we do have much to consider from the history of the Alpha forerunner. And, as a knowledge of acorns is helpful in understanding oak trees, we can—if we make the effort—form a surprisingly detailed picture of the Omega.

So, let us consider the Alpha.

---

15   *Selected Messages*, Book One, 200

16   *Selected Messages*, Book One, 203

Chapter Two
The Alpha and the Omega

AS mentioned in the previous chapter, the "pantheism" portion of the "Kellogg crisis" began with the writing of *The Living Temple* and reached something of a climax about a year and a half later at the Autumn Council of 1903. One more unfortunately divisive consideration of the issue occurred at the Lake Union Conference meeting held at Berrien Springs in the spring of 1904. This was perhaps the last "half decent" chance to salvage the church's working relationship with Dr. Kellogg. As such, it is of keen interest to historians, but it doesn't provide a great deal more information for our consideration, which will focus primarily on the nature of the Alpha as a means of understanding the Omega.

For the sake of clarity, here is an outline of the characteristics of the Alpha that we will consider in five short chapters:

1. The Alpha was subtle enough to be largely unrecognized as a concern. Dr. Kellogg did and said many good things, and in these areas he was strongly supported by Ellen White, sometimes in the face of direct opposition by other individuals and groups within the church. It is easy to understand, then, how those who tended to appreciate the doctor might overlook his errors. But the subtlety of the Alpha went further than that, and many who did not support Kellogg's work where they should have were also blinded to the dangerous positions he took.

2. The views presented by Dr. Kellogg—both in his book, *The Living Temple*, and in his public and private statements to others—presented God as "in" all created things. This perspective undermined the natural reading of the Bible which presents God as a distinct personage. These ideas, while often hailed as spiritually inspiring, were very short on fact and detail. On the whole, they tended to be quite nebulous, leaving no solid "truth" on which to build any concept of God,

heaven, or the plan of salvation. In contrast, Ellen White consistently presented the teachings of the Bible as clear and specific.

3. Ellen White repeatedly remarked that the teachings of the Alpha were similar to errors and heresies she had had to meet in the very early years of her ministry. One common element she often cited was a tendency toward sensuality and "free-lovism." To Ellen White, these errors were significant. They were, in fact, a deadly threat to spiritual life. So much so, that the Lord's messenger called repeatedly for parents to *not* allow their children to be lured to Battle Creek by the promise of a medical education.

4. Proponents of the Alpha teachings repeatedly tried to equate their positions with the teachings of Ellen White. This assertion she adamantly denied, which left Kellogg and his allies in the position of either entirely rejecting the Spirit of Prophecy (which they were reluctant to do since the Adventist Church was a major source of funding for them), or of explaining away certain portions of her writings while professing to accept others.

5. The Spirit of Prophecy speaks of Kellogg's teaching as "spiritualistic," both in the sense of "spiritualizing away" the truths of the Bible, and also in the sense of involving the direct agency of demonic forces.

The purpose of this historical review is not simply history, of course. On the strength of Ellen White's linkage of the Alpha of the past with the Omega of the future, the value lies in what we might learn about the identification of the latter, and the proper response to it. Anything we can gain here, will be an asset as we consider more recent developments in the remainder of the book.

Chapter Three
Subtle Like a Snake

SURPRISING as it may seem, low-level pantheism didn't raise a lot of red flags when it first walked into the Adventist church. One of the first clear instances was in a series of sermons by Dr. Kellogg at the General Conference session of 1897. Here is his introduction to one of the sermons, describing a change of understanding that he said had come to him in recent years:

> I was trying to believe in God and nature. I had two gods. But I could not go on thus. I could not see how God could be above nature, so I had taken the position that God was not above nature. I had only a glimpse of the truth. I was in great perplexity; I did not know that God was in nature; so I believed that nature was almost equal with God. ... I did not see how God could be higher than nature; but I had been taught that God is one thing, and nature another thing. But when I found out that God was in nature, I thought of it in a different light.[17]

Another example:

> This expression, "the image of God," means that God put into the mass of clay, out of which man was made, everything of God that it is possible to manifest through the human form. Adam was created in the first place in the image of God, a perfect man. Adam fell—wandered away from God. Again "God manifest in the flesh," appeared in Christ, the second Adam. In Christ we have the same sort of an image of God that we had in the first Adam. We are apt to think of Christ as possessed of a divinity absolutely different in kind from what we find anywhere else except in God; but as there is only one God, there is only one kind of divinity; and as Christ was divine, wherever we find the image of God we find the same

---

17   *General Conference Daily Bulletin*, February 18, 1897, 72

divinity. Christ was divine in an unmeasurably larger and more perfect sense than man, and yet we have in man the same image of God and the same divinity as in Christ. Christ was a perfect man. Adam, as God made him, was a perfect man. Man now, as we find him, is not perfect. Man's perfection was in his divinity. ...

The same divinity that was in Christ is in us. [18]

To anyone sensitized to pantheism, this doesn't look good at all. But, on the other hand, neither is it full blown Hinduism. Somehow it all managed to pass as some sort of new insight that was kind of exciting.

One reason Kellogg was never challenged for saying this sort of thing was that he wasn't the only one expressing such ideas. Though not as blatant, the words of W.W. Prescott were still less than clear:

God makes us alive simply by giving us his own life. ... As he reveals that life in our experience day by day by simply living in us, we stand still, as it were, and see it go on. [19]

Prescott seems to have gotten his fascination with *"life"* from E.J. Waggoner, with whom he had worked closely while in England. During his time there, Waggoner had occasionally written thoughts such as these:

The air that we breathe, the water that we drink, the food that we eat, the light that we enjoy, is full of life, wonderful life. The grass and herbs and trees live and grow. Multitudes of creatures great and small live in the sea; beasts and creeping things live on the dry land; and birds and insects live in the air. ...

Where does all this power and life come from? Not from the creatures themselves, for they cannot keep themselves alive one moment. ... There is One with whom is the fountain of all this life, from whom flows the life of every living thing, and the breath of all mankind. [20]

---

18   *General Conference Daily Bulletin*, February 18, 1897, 77–78

19   *General Conference Daily Bulletin*, February 26, 1897, 165

20   *The Present Truth* [UK], February 15, 1894, 109

We take in the life of Jesus in our food, drink it in the water, breathe it in the air, and receive it in the life-giving sunlight. As the leaf and the branch live in the tree and by the life of the tree, so "in Him we live, and move, and have our being," and so does everything that lives and moves, as much the tiny insect and frail blossom, as all the great works of His hands.[21]

This idea of fully equating life in the creation with the life of the Creator eventually grew to the point that by 1899 Ellen White would write:

Letters have come to me, asking in regard to the teaching of some who say that nothing that has life should be killed, not even insects, however annoying or distressing they may be. Is it possible that anyone claims that God has given him this message to give to the people? The Lord has never given any human being such a message. God has told no one that it is a sin to kill the insects which destroy our peace and rest. In all His teaching, Christ gave no message of this character, and His disciples are to teach only what He commanded them.[22]

Over time, the emphasis on "the life of God in everything and everyone" evolved into an emphasis on the expected evidence of the power of that life in the obedient believer. The expectation of great and miraculous results had led to an unhealthy spiritual enthusiasm. Stephen Haskell wrote to tell Ellen White (who was still in Australia at this time) some of the specifics that were being taught by different ministers scattered about the United States. In reply, she wrote a lengthy letter of which we can only look at brief excerpts:

I have just read your letters, and I will now try to write to you. The things of which you write are simply foolish imaginings which are presented to the people. The teachers who cherish them need to learn anew the principles of our faith. They need to be thoroughly converted. To make the statements they make, and hold the notions they hold, is like descending from

---

21 *The Present Truth* [UK], June 15, 1899, 378

22 *Selected Messages*, Book One, 170

the highest elevation to which the truth of the Word takes men, to the lowest level. God is not working with such men. Having lost the grand truths of the Word of God, which center in the third angel's message. ...

Those who cherish and advocate fanciful ideas need to be taught what is truth before they attempt to teach others. Man-made theories and suppositions are not to be allowed to enter the work. But do not give the impression that there are many who are going to foolish extremes. There are a few ill-balanced minds that are ready to catch at anything of a sensational character. But I tell you that there are many in America who are as true as steel to principle, and these will be helped and blessed, for they are weeping between the porch and the altar, saying, "Spare Thy people, O Lord, and give not Thine heritage to reproach" [Joel 2:17]. ...

Those who present the idea that the blind, the deaf, the lame, the deformed, will not receive the seal of God, are not speaking words given them by the Holy Spirit. There is much suffering in our world. To some, suffering and disease have been transmitted as an inheritance. Others suffer because of accidents. Cause and effect are always in operation in our world, and always will be. The Lord has afflicted ones, dearly beloved in His sight, who bear the suffering of bodily infirmities. To them special care and grace is promised. Their trials will not be greater than they can endure. ...

The Lord Jesus did not bring forth any of the cheap suppositions that some who claim to be teachers are manufacturing. There can be no value in the fables that are composed by guesswork to make an impression on minds. Young men must be educated to keep within the bounds of "It is written.". ...

No one is to put truth to the torture by cheap imaginings, by putting a forced, mystical construction upon the Word. ...

Satan is well pleased when he can thus confuse the mind. Let not ministers preach their own suppositions. Let them search the Scriptures earnestly, with a solemn realization that if they teach for doctrine the things that are not contained in God's Word, they will be as those represented in the last chapter of Revelation. ...

In the Word there are the most precious ideas. These will be secured by those who study with earnestness, for heavenly angels will direct the search; but the angels never lead the mind to dwell upon cheap nonsense, as though it were the Word of God. ...

In God's Word the question is not, What is the color of the hair or the form of the body? but, Has the heart been purified, made white, and tried? [23]

The point of importance here is the manner in which these "pantheism lite" doctrines developed. This one idea of a closer relationship with the Lord through an understanding of His life within all life, carelessly worded, imaginatively expanded, and enthusiastically presented as "advanced" truth, gradually made its way into the preaching of about four or five prominent Adventist ministers, and was no doubt reflected to some degree in the musings of many less well known church workers. One final example will suffice: In the General Conference session of 1899, Dr. E.J. Waggoner gave a sermon entitled, "The Water of Life." In this sermon Waggoner repeatedly mixes up things real, and things figurative:

"Spiritual things are spiritually discerned." If we were there at the side of the throne, some would see the river, and some would not see it. He who has his eyesight trained to discern spiritual things would see the stream flowing. The man who is not spiritual would not see anything. One might say, "O, I see the bright and sparkling water flowing from the throne of God;" and another would reply, "I can not see it." Did you ever hear people say, "I can not see it"? When a man can not see, what is the matter with him?—He is blind. Then, "I counsel thee to buy of me gold tried in the fire, ... and anoint thine eyes with eye-salve, that thou mayest see"—not to be blind.

---

23 *Manuscript Releases*, vol. 14, 55–61

Whether or not it was actually so, this passage makes it look like Waggoner could hardly tell the difference between the real and the symbolic. The message to Laodicea is *not* a prescription to treat the loss of one's literal, physical eyesight! But it gets worse:

> O, I delight in drinking water, as I never have before; I delight in bathing. Why, I come right to the throne of God. A man may get righteousness in bathing, when he knows where the water comes from, and recognizes the source. The world is a good deal nearer the gospel than it knows anything about when it says that "cleanliness is next to godliness." Ah, but cleanliness is godliness. "Now ye are clean through the word which I have spoken unto you." Christ loved the church, and gave himself for it, that he might purify it and cleanse it by a "water-bath in the word." That is the way it reads in the Danish, and that is literal, too. Just bathe in the word. That is not figurative, that is not sentimental; God wants his people to live now as seeing the Invisible, so that they will walk in the sight of the river of God, and drink from the throne of God, and all they do will be eating and drinking in his presence. [24]

You'll notice that these last two quotations are from the 1899 General Conference session. Interestingly enough, Ellen White—living in Australia at the time—sent a manuscript to that session to be read publicly. The title was, "The True Relation of God and Nature," and it plainly stated that:

> Nature is not God, and never was God. The voice of nature testifies of God, declaring his glory; but nature itself is not God. As God's created work, it but bears a testimony of his power. [25]

None of this is meant to demean anyone, but it's important to understand that Dr. Kellogg was surrounded by these ideas, for all of them found their way to Battle Creek (and some of them originated there). And there was another, possibly even more influential source

---

24 *General Conference Daily Bulletin*, February 24, 1899, 79–80

25 *General Conference Daily Bulletin*, March 6, 1899

for Kellogg's pantheistic views. We turn again to the recollections of Dr. S.P.S. Edwards for this part of the story:

> One day a white-bearded gentleman came in [to my classroom at Battle Creek College] and took a seat with the class. It was A.H. Lewis, D.D., LL.D., etc., the editor of the *Sabbath Recorder*, church paper of the Seventh Day Baptists. … After the class Dr. Lewis came over and shook hands and said, "You gave a wonderful talk to your class. Is this not an unusual approach to a scientific subject like physiology?… Doctor, do you not think that you may be stretching a point, in emphasizing the exact features of God's being? He is a spirit. You talk of His hands, His feet and eyes and ears and tongue just like He were a physical being. God is a presence, an essence; He is everywhere, in the trees, in the flowers, the food we eat. Are you not in danger of getting too narrow a view of God?"

> After a minute's thought, I answered, "Admitting for the time being what you have said about God, to me He has hands; He holds my hand. He has feet; I walk in His footsteps. He has ears; He hears my prayers. He has eyes; He sees my sins and forgives them, my weakness and gives me strength, my heart yearning and gives me grace. God is a person to me."

> The discussion ended with my having learned where Dr. Kellogg, George Fifield, W.W. Prescott, M. Bessie DeGraw, and E.J. Waggoner got some, if not much of their pantheism. Dr. Lewis was once Mrs. Kellogg's pastor and president of Alfred University, where she got her degree. His paper, the *Sabbath Recorder*, was steeped in pantheism. It came regularly to the Kellogg home. George Fifield's book, *God Is Love* is as strongly pantheistic as *Living Temple*. He was closely tied to the Seventh Day Baptists and when dropped by the Seventh-day Adventists he became the pastor of the Seventh Day Baptist church in Battle Creek of which Dr. Kellogg was a member.

> I personally was taught more pantheism by W.W. Prescott than by Dr. Kellogg. I never believed or taught it, but was the target

for repeated talks and studies by Professor and Mrs. Prescott for several years before 1904. Never after that.

Here is the connection: Professor Prescott and Dr. E.J. Waggoner were in London for years in the 1890s. I have good evidence that while there they were closely associated with the Seventh Day Baptists who were an old established body in England. They both came back to the U.S. in 1900 strongly indoctrinated with pantheism, and, knowing of my teaching in the college along spiritual lines, they made desperate attempts, repeatedly, to get me to follow their line in my teaching. ...

From this you must gather that, to my certain knowledge, Dr. Kellogg was not alone in going astray on some doctrinal points. He and some of his immediate associates were the only ones who got the blame and refused to recant. [26]

Edwards' memory wasn't perfect—Lewis was chairman of the Church History and Homiletics department at the Seventh Day Baptist Alfred University, but never president. Mrs. Kellogg, a lifelong Seventh Day Baptist, had graduated from Alfred University in 1872, and completed her M.A. degree there in 1885, so the Kelloggs' association with Lewis was a long-term affair. [27] But of more importance for us at the moment are Edwards' general observations about Kellogg and the others.

Edwards sounds almost defensive of Dr. Kellogg, so it should be noted that he never seeks to excuse Kellogg's pantheism. [28] As Edwards said, the key difference between Kellogg and the others was that Kellogg refused to honestly recant of his teaching, and the same

---

26   Sanford P.S. Edwards, *Memoirs of SDA Pioneers*, 9–10

27   Another point of concern is that, in his youth, Lewis had been a spiritualist medium, "after the rude manner of those times." Had he given it up? Or just become more sophisticated? See *Hindsight: Seventh-day Adventist History in Essays and Extracts*, 171

28   Edwards genuinely liked Kellogg, and considered him a good—though seriously flawed—friend. Kellogg had taken an interest in Edwards when, as a young man, he had arrived in Battle Creek with $16 and the determination to become a physician. Over the years, Kellogg had assisted, taken advantage of, defended, and opposed Edwards as circumstances and issues had come and gone, but Edwards held no personal grudge.

might be said of many other issues which had strained his relationship with the church.

Others did repent, and that's a big difference. We can be thankful for the work of Ellen White in this regard, for there were few others who saw the problem, and fewer still who were prepared to speak up about it. Were it not for her sermons, letters, and one-on-one conversations with men like Dr. David Paulson, Dr. Daniel Kress, W.W. Prescott, E.A. Sutherland, and P.T. Magan, the church would most likely have lost many more talented workers.

But our focus at the moment is that, even though many should have raised the alarm over pantheism, no one did:

I have some things to say to our teachers in reference to the new book, *The Living Temple*. Be careful how you sustain the sentiments of this book regarding the personality of God. As the Lord represents matters to me, these sentiments do not bear the endorsement of God. They are a snare that the enemy has prepared for these last days. I thought that this would surely be discerned, and that it would not be necessary for me to say anything about it. But since the claim has been made that the teachings of this book can be sustained by statements from my writings, I am compelled to speak in denial of this claim. [29]

In a representation which passed before me, I saw a certain work being done by medical missionary workers. Our ministering brethren were looking on, watching what was being done, but they did not seem to understand. The foundation of our faith, which was established by so much prayer, such earnest searching of the Scriptures, was being taken down, pillar by pillar. Our faith was to have nothing to rest upon—the sanctuary

---

Years later he would write, "You might think I am somewhat partial to Dr. Kellogg. Why should I not be? I owe him much. ... I respected him, and loved him, in spite of his faults. I know many more faults than I will tell, for he was my friend. I am glad to get that on paper; I have wanted to say it for a long time." *Memoirs of SDA Pioneers*, 15

Perhaps the angel Gabriel has similarly mixed memories of a superior he once served under.

29 *Review and Herald*, October 22, 1903

was gone, the atonement was gone. I realized that something must be done.

The battle nearly killed me. I saw what was coming in, and I saw that our brethren were blind. They did not realize the danger. Our young people, especially, were in danger. They delighted in the beautiful representation—God in the flower, God in the leaf, God in the tree. But if God be in these things, why not worship them? [30]

To Ellen White, the most discouraging aspect of all this was likely the thought that individuals long trusted in responsible positions within the church and her institutions should have proven blind to the dangers that were threatening the people of God.

To me it seems passing strange that some who have been long in the work of God cannot discern the character of the teaching in *Living Temple* in regard to God. [31]

The sentiments in *Living Temple* regarding the personality of God have been received even by men who have had a long experience in the truth. When such men consent to eat of the fruit of the tree of knowledge of good and evil, we are no longer to regard the subject as a matter to be treated with the greatest delicacy. That those whom we thought sound in the faith should have failed to discern the specious, deadly influence of this science of evil, should alarm us as nothing else has alarmed us.

It is something that can not be treated as a small matter that men who have had so much light, and such clear evidence as to the genuineness of the truth we hold, should become unsettled, and led to accept spiritualistic theories regarding the personality of God. [32]

---

30 *Sermons and Talks*, vol. 1, 344

31 *Manuscript Releases*, vol. 11, 314

32 *Special Testimonies* Series B, No. 7, 37

The Alpha was subtle, so subtle that almost no one paid any attention to it. The influence of one influential person (Dr. Kellogg) seemed to carry many others along without them even realizing they were leaving the gospel of Christ behind. With multiple individuals—many of whom meant well, and were eventually salvaged for the Lord's work—repeating the same ideas, heresy took on the appearance of accepted truth.

But it wasn't truth, and only when Ellen White began to speak up did it begin to dawn on some of the actors in the drama that they were hurting the cause of God. We might have expected her to be furious with them. After all, they *should have known better!* And yet, we find her—year after year—pleading for their souls, seeking any and every means to draw their hearts back to God, and their footsteps away from impending disaster.

That was the "Alpha"; will there be parallels in the "Omega"?

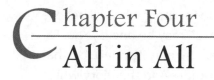

Chapter Four
All in All

MUCH of the confusion and error of the Alpha came, at its most basic level, from a misunderstanding and misapplication of the idea of God being "in" something or someone. Lest there be any thought that this is just a simple case of "use the dictionary to find out what the word means," we'll begin with a look at a Bible passage often quoted by Ellen White:

> I do not pray for the world but for those whom You have given Me, for they are Yours. And all Mine are Yours, and Yours are Mine, and I am glorified in them.

> Now I am no longer in the world, but these are in the world, and I come to You. Holy Father, keep through Your name those whom You have given Me, that they may be one as We are. While I was with them in the world, I kept them in Your name. Those whom You gave Me I have kept; and none of them is lost except the son of perdition, that the Scripture might be fulfilled. But now I come to You, and these things I speak in the world, that they may have My joy fulfilled in themselves. I have given them Your word; and the world has hated them because they are not of the world, just as I am not of the world.

If there is anything clear in this passage so far, it is that Jesus—in His last prayer with His disciples before the crucifixion—was making a distinction between them and the world. Even Judas is carefully specified as not being a member of the company which Jesus has kept in the Father's name. The disciples, of course, did not understand the true condition of "the son of perdition" at that time, but Jesus did.

And yet Jesus was not content with a prayer for only eleven confused and soon-to-be-demoralized men:

> I do not pray for these alone, but also for those who will believe in Me through their word; that they all may be one, as You, Father, are in Me, and I in You; that they also may be one in Us, that the world may believe that You sent Me. And the glory which You gave Me I have given them, that they may be one just as We are one: I in them, and You in Me; that they may be made perfect in one, and that the world may know that You have sent Me, and have loved them as You have loved Me. ... And I have declared to them Your name, and will declare it, that the love with which You loved Me may be in them, and I in them. [33]

This prayer of Christ's took in not only the disciples then living, but all who would believe down to the end of time. And what was Jesus' petition? In this final outpouring of prayer, what did He ask of His Father? That His disciples might be one "in Us"; that Jesus might be "in them"; that they might be made perfect; and that through all this, the world might see evidence testifying to the validity of Christ's mission.

This prayer is important for many reasons, but our interest just now is the unique position of the disciples, those whom Jesus prayed to be "in." There is no ambiguity here. Christ is to be "in" those who believe, those who give evidence of the work He was sent from heaven to do.

One basic confusion of the Alpha was the idea that God was indiscriminately "in" *all* His creation. This is why insects came to be regarded as "sacred cows" and taking a bath was supposed to be such a great thing. But it was, after all, just fanciful theories and faulty speculation:

> I have been instructed by the heavenly messenger that some of the reasoning in the book *Living Temple* is unsound, and that this reasoning would lead astray the minds of those who are not thoroughly established on the foundation principles of present truth. It introduces that which is naught but speculation in regard to the personality of God and where His presence is. No one on this earth has a right to speculate on this question. The

---

33   John 17:9–23, 26

more fanciful theories are discussed, the less men will know of God and of the truth that sanctifies the soul.

One and another come to me, asking me to explain the positions taken in *Living Temple*. I reply, "They are unexplainable." The sentiments expressed do not give a true knowledge of God. All through the book are passages of Scripture. These scriptures are brought in in such a way that error is made to appear as truth. Erroneous theories are presented in so pleasing a way that unless care is taken, many will be misled. [34]

One of the most peculiar facets of the Alpha experience was the sometimes childish fascination shown for insignificant thoughts. Marveling over the sanctification obtained in a bathtub seems—well, kind of silly. But it's really nothing much different than the reverential awe shown for the birth of an albino buffalo, or the thrill of a Wiccan marking the winter solstice. The event is only significant if one believes in some enhanced or extended meaning—the buffalo is prophetic, or the solstice brings greater opportunity for communion with Mother Goddess. Only the believer is capable of such awe, and so it was in the Alpha.

I am instructed to say, The sentiments of those who are searching for advanced scientific ideas are not to be trusted. Such representations as the following are made: "The Father is as the light invisible; the Son is as the light embodied; the Spirit is the light shed abroad." "The Father is like the dew, invisible vapor; the Son is like the dew gathered in beauteous form; the Spirit is like the dew fallen to the seat of life." Another representation: "The Father is like the invisible vapor; the Son is like the leaden cloud; the Spirit is rain fallen and working in refreshing power."

All these spiritualistic representations are simply nothingness. They are imperfect, untrue. They weaken and diminish the Majesty which no earthly likeness can be compared to. God can not be compared with the things His hands have made. These are mere earthly things, suffering under the curse of God because of

---

34   *Selected Messages*, Book One, 201–202

the sins of man. The Father can not be described by the things of earth. The Father is all the fullness of the Godhead bodily, and is invisible to mortal sight. [35]

What would persuade anyone to be impressed with pointless musings about light and water? It's one thing if it's a metaphor for something clearly understandable and communicated from an intelligent source. When Jesus spoke of the "water of life," He certainly did not intend anyone to rhapsodize over an eight ounce glass. The *thought* was significant; the image, the metaphor, was simply a communication device. But in the "representations" Ellen White cites above, there is no promise, no instruction, no prophecy, no nothing! It's just "The Father is as the light invisible." What is *that* supposed to mean? Ultraviolet? Infrared? And what does it *do* for anyone?

In this book there are statements that the writer himself does not comprehend. Many things are stated in a vague, undefined way. Statements are made in such a way that nothing is sure.[36]

It would appear that it was a case of "The Emperor's New Philosophy." There was no benefit to come through *understanding* the philosophy; the benefit was supposed to just magically accrue to all who *accepted* the philosophy. And what was the benefit? Since God was in *everything*, then He must be within *every* person. Perhaps by having God "within," salvation could seem almost assured. How long would it take to go from that position to rank universalism? Apparently, not long.

To those who would represent every man as born a king; to those who would make no distinction between the converted and the unconverted; to those who are losing their appreciation of their need of Christ as their Saviour, I would say, Think of yourselves as you have been during the period of your existence! Would it be pleasant or agreeable for you to contemplate feature after feature of your life work, in the sight of Him who knows every thought of man, and before Whose eyes all man's doings are as an open book?

---

35 *Special Testimonies*, Series B, No. 7, 62

36 *Review and Herald*, October 22, 1903

In other words, mysticism doesn't affect the judgment! There is still an objective reality with which all must deal. We may *wish* we were all born with "divinity within," but we aren't. We may *wish* that our feelings could decide our eternal destiny, but they won't. How did such deceptions ever come into God's Remnant Church?

I call upon all who are engaged in the service of God to place themselves fully on Christ's side. There are dangers on the right and on the left. Our greatest danger will come from men who have lifted up their souls unto vanity, who have not heeded the words of warning and reproof sent them by God. As such men choose their own will and way, the tempter, clothed in angel robes, is close beside them, ready to unite his influence with theirs. He opens to them delusions of a most attractive character, which they present to the people of God. Some of those who listen to them will be deceived, and will work in dangerous lines. ...

Well, then, what are we *supposed* to do? Ellen White continues:

The one book that is essential for all to study is the Bible. Studied with reverence and godly fear, it is the greatest of all educators. In it there is no sophistry. Its pages are filled with truth. Would you gain a knowledge of God and Christ, whom He sent into the world to live and die for sinners? An earnest, diligent study of the Bible is necessary in order to gain this knowledge. [37]

Her point is quite simple, really. Mysticism may offer beautifully attractive concepts, but reality still wins out. What we think, doesn't change the universe around us (even though the idea that it will is a popular belief). The "unsound" "fanciful theories" and "foolish imaginings" of mysticism are "unexplainable." They may be enticing, but they aren't true, which is to say that they simply don't describe reality. If you want truth, remember what Jesus said: "Your word is truth." [38]

---

37   *Loma Linda Messages*, 64

38   John 17:17

And if you want a catchy sound bite for distinguishing truth from mysticism, try

Heaven is not a vapor. It is a place. [39]

And one final quotation to consider, with a little fringe benefit. The focus on Scripture remains as always, but notice the comment on meditation—"diligent" is not a companion word to "mindless."

The world is to be taken captive by Satan's deceiving representations. Where then is our security? How shall we guard against Satan's bewitching artifices? By reading the Word of God with an intensity of desire to know Him in the light of [the] revelation which He has left on record of Himself; by meditating upon His precepts diligently. We are to obey His commands, afraid to venture out of the path of divine revelation, and to indulge in fallacious reasoning. [40]

That was the "Alpha"; will there be parallels in the "Omega"?

---

39 *Manuscript Releases*, vol. 4, 60

40 *Special Testimonies*, Series B, No. 7, 50

Chapter Five
Unrighteous Reruns

WHEN Ellen White read excerpts from *The Living Temple* for the first time, it had a familiar ring to it. She told the story this way:

About the time that *Living Temple* was published, there passed before me in the night season, representations indicating that some danger was approaching, and that I must prepare for it by writing out the things God had revealed to me regarding the foundation principles of our faith. A copy of *Living Temple* was sent me, but it remained in my library, unread. From the light given me by the Lord, I knew that some of the sentiments advocated in the book did not bear the endorsement of God, and that they were a snare that the enemy had prepared for the last days. I thought that this would surely be discerned, and that it would not be necessary for me to say anything about it.

In the controversy that arose among our brethren regarding the teachings of this book, those in favor of giving it a wide circulation declared: "It contains the very sentiments that Sister White has been teaching." This assertion struck right to my heart. I felt heartbroken; for I knew that this representation of the matter was not true.

Finally my son said to me, "Mother, you ought to read at least some parts of the book, that you may see whether they are in harmony with the light that God has given you." He sat down beside me, and together we read the preface, and most of the first chapter, and also paragraphs in other chapters. As we read, I recognized the very sentiments against which I had been bidden to speak in warning during the early days of my public labors. When I first left the State of Maine, it was to go through

Vermont and Massachusetts, to bear a testimony against these sentiments.[41]

This link to her early experience was not a passing connection in her mind. She commented on it several times, with interesting details and perspectives in each account. Because of this, we'll quote several of these passages at considerable length:

After the passing of the time, we were opposed and cruelly falsified. Erroneous theories were pressed in upon us by men and women who had gone into fanaticism. I was directed to go to the places where these people were advocating these erroneous theories. … Just such theories as you have presented in *Living Temple* were presented then. These subtle, deceiving sophistries have again and again sought to find place among us. But I have ever had the same testimony to bear which I now bear regarding the personality of God.[42]

Ever since I was seventeen years old, I have had to fight this battle against false theories, in defense of the truth. The history of our past experience is indelibly fixed in my mind and I am determined that no theories of the order that you have been accepting shall come into our ranks.[43]

In the early days of the message, I have passed through most trying ordeals in refuting false doctrines, and especially such doctrines as Pantheism [which] we are meeting now. We are passing over the same ground.[44]

These heresies are similar to those that I met in my first labors in connection with the cause in Maine, New Hampshire, Vermont, then in Boston, Roxbury, New Bedford, and other parts of Massachusetts. Through them the evil one worked upon the minds of men and women.

---

41 *Selected Messages*, Book One, 202–203

42 *Manuscript Releases*, vol. 4, 57

43 *Manuscript Releases*, vol. 4, 60

44 *Manuscript Releases*, vol. 4, 248

There was a Mrs. Minor, who had been to Jerusalem. When she returned she advocated some of these sentimental, spiritualistic sophistries. She invited me to visit her and relate what the Lord shown me. Brother Nichols took my sister and self to her home in Roxbury, where we found a company of about twenty assembled. Among them were brethren and sisters whom I loved and highly esteemed. They had believed the testimonies that I had borne to the people. But they had been led astray by spiritualistic ideas which were nothing less than a love-sick sentimentalism. The power of God came upon me as I warned them of their dangers, and some said they had never expected to see so much of the blessing of God this side of the Eden above. I bore them a message similar to the message I have been bearing for the last two months. I was instructed that the ideas they had accepted were but the alpha of a great deception. I had to meet similar delusions in Portsmouth and in Boston.

These doctrines led to free-loveism, and my heart was sorely grieved as I saw the result they brought to those who accepted them. One family who for years had lived happily together was broken up. A man and his wife, well advanced in years, were separated. The husband left his wife and children, and established other family relations. We seemed to be able to do nothing to break the spell upon these persons. The precious truths of the Bible had no influence over them. [45]

Had God desired to be represented as dwelling personally in the things of nature—in the flower, the tree, the spear of grass—would not Christ have spoken of this to His disciples? To take the works of God, and represent them to be God, is a fearful misrepresentation. This misrepresentation of God I was called upon to oppose at the beginning of my work, when the Lord sent me forth to proclaim the message that He should give me to speak.

My labors on this line began when I was seventeen years old, and since then I have been over the ground again and again. Case

---

45 *Manuscript Releases*, vol. 11, 248

after case has been presented to me, and the power of God has rested on me as I have stood before large assemblies and called out the names of those who were entertaining false views, telling them where such views would lead them if they did not change.

I have seen the results of these fanciful views of God in apostasy, spiritualism, free-lovism. The free-love tendencies of these teachings were so concealed that it was difficult to present them in their real character. Until the Lord presented it to me I knew not what to call it, but I was instructed to call it unholy spiritual love.

I am warned that we are not to talk of God as He is spoken of in *Living Temple*. The sentiments there expressed are a dishonor to His greatness and His majesty. God forbid that our ministers should entertain these ideas. For myself, I take my stand firmly against them. And I entreat you to accept the message that I bear to you. I ask you to arouse to your danger. Who by searching can find out God?

The theory that He is an essence, pervading everything, is one of Satan's most subtle devices. I warn you to beware of being led to accept theories leading to any such view. I tell you, my brother, that the most spiritual-minded Christians are liable to be deceived by these beautiful, seducing, flattering theories. But in the place of honoring God, these theories, in the minds of those who receive them, bring Him down to a low level, where He is nothingness. [46]

I am so sorry that *Living Temple* came out as it did, and was circulated, and the worst of it—that which struck right to my heart—was the assertion made regarding the book: "It contains the very sentiments that Sister White has been teaching." When I heard this, I felt so heartbroken that it seemed as if I could not say anything. Had I said anything, I would have been obliged to speak the truth as it was.

---

46 *Manuscript Releases*, vol. 21, 172

Representations had been shown me that some danger was approaching, and that I must prepare for it. I must write out the things God had given me in order to prepare for it.

I did not read *Living Temple*, though I had it in my library. At last my son said to me, "Mother, you ought to read at least some parts of the book, that you may see whether they are in harmony with the light that God has given you." He sat down beside me, and we read the paragraphs to which he referred. When we had finished I turned to him and said, "These are the very sentiments against which I was bidden to speak in warning at the very beginning of my public work. When I first left the State of Maine, it was to go through Vermont and Massachusetts, to bear a testimony against these sentiments. *Living Temple* contains the Alpha of these theories. The Omega would follow in a little while. I tremble for our people. These beautiful representations are similar to the temptation that the enemy brought to Adam and Eve in Eden.

When but a girl I went to New Hampshire to bear warning against these same doctrines. There was a man by the name of Billings and another by the name of Bennet who were preaching a higher spirituality. I was asked to meet these men, and I did so, giving them the light that God had given me. In the meeting a great distress came upon me. I was taken off in vision. The men began to triumph, thinking that things were going their way. When I got up to bear my testimony, they began to shout. I stopped and did not say a word until they had finished. Then I went on and told them plainly where the doctrines they were advocating would lead to.

I met these same doctrines in Dorchester, Mass., where for a time I made my home. In one meeting held there a man arose and after making a confession, said, "I have listened today to the testimony of Ellen Harmon, and I feel as if I had been partaking of the richest feast ever set before me." In the past this man had been a model of piety, but these seductive theories came before him—theories teaching that men and women could live above all sin—and he accepted them. What was the result? He left his wife and children and went to live with another woman.

I was at this time nothing but a girl, and I said, "Why am I left to bear this testimony?" Said the one in whose house I was staying, "God knows why. The men advocating these doctrines have a strong influence as being very pious men, and if we were to say anything against them, they would put us in prison. But you are a minor, and they cannot touch you."

We met these theories again in Topsham, Maine. A brother there, who had accepted them, was very sick, and he wanted me to pray for him. I said, "I cannot pray for you so long as you and these sisters are so free with one another." He sent for Elder James White, who, when he came, asked him, "What are you going to do?" "Do!" he said, "Do you ask what I am going to do? I am going to cut loose from all these evils. I am going to take my stand in harmony with what Sister Ellen Harmon has been presenting to me. I accept what she has said as the word of the Lord." Thus the company with which he was connected was broken up. And many more such companies were broken up by the light that God gave me.

Thus I worked and suffered in my girlhood. And all through my life I have had the same errors to meet, though not always in the same form. In *Living Temple* the assertion is made that God is in the flower, in the leaf, in the sinner. But God does not live in the sinner. The Word declares that He abides only in the hearts of those who love Him and do righteousness. God does not abide in the heart of the sinner; it is the enemy who abides there.

There are some things upon which we must reason, and there are other things that we must not discuss. In regard to God— what He is and where He is—silence is eloquence. When you are tempted to speak of what God is, keep silence, because as surely as you begin to speak of this, you will disparage Him.

Our ministers must be very careful not to enter into controversy in regard to the personality of God. This is a subject that they are not to touch. It is a mystery, and the enemy will surely lead astray those who enter into it. We know that Christ came in person to reveal God to the world. God is a person and Christ is a person. Christ is spoken of in the Word as "the brightness of His Father's glory, and the express image of His person."

I was forbidden to talk with Dr. Kellogg on this subject, because it is not a subject to be talked about. And I was instructed that certain sentiments in *Living Temple* were the Alpha of a long list of deceptive theories. [47]

Surprisingly, this aspect of Ellen White's reaction to *Living Temple* has not been commonly considered in most discussions of the subject. Since there are quite a number of points which help fill out our understanding, let's note them in detail. First, here's a list of terms Ellen White used to describe the teachings of Dr. Kellogg and the other individuals from earlier experiences:

- sentiments; erroneous theories; fanaticism; subtle, deceiving sophistries; false theories; false doctrines; pantheism; heresies; sentimental, spiritualistic sophistries; spiritualistic ideas which were nothing less than a love-sick sentimentalism; great deception; free-loveism; fearful misrepresentation; false views; fanciful views; free-love tendencies; unholy spiritual love; theory that He is an essence, pervading everything; beautiful, seducing, flattering theories; beautiful representations... similar to the temptation that the enemy brought to Adam and Eve; theories teaching that men and women could live above all sin; same errors... though not always in the same form; assertion... that God is in the flower, in the leaf, in the sinner; not a subject to be talked about; the Alpha of a long list of deceptive theories.

It's quite a list! A bit overwhelming, perhaps, so let's try to break it down into a number of general categories.

- Adjectives indicating error, such as false, heresies, misrepresentation, and erroneous.
- Terms indicating deceit, such as deceiving sophistries, deception, unholy, seducing, flattering, temptation, and with an implied pejorative sense, theories and assertion.

---

47 *Sermons and Talks*, vol. 1, 343

- Illustrative terms such as pantheism, sentimental, spiritualistic, love-sick sentimentalism, free-lovism, unholy spiritual love, the direct comparison to the temptation in Eden, and theories about living above all sin.

No doubt we might find more terms that could fit in this list if we were to go back and look at the accounts of all those earlier episodes, but this is enough to work with for now. The first category—adjectives indicating error—is almost self-evident. We already know she's talking about errors.

The second category—deceit—adds a glimpse behind the scenes, so that we can see the agency of Satan working determinedly against God's people.

The final category is perhaps the most interesting. The association between "pantheism" (as commonly conceived) and sentimentalism, free-lovism, and mistaken ideas of sanctification is not always obvious. Perhaps we needn't feel too dense in this regard; even Ellen White "knew not what to call it" until she was "instructed."

But this less-than-obvious connection is consistently specified in Ellen White's various accounts. This is not a fluke relationship; it's something inherent in the deception. Particularly notable on this third list is the comment about "theories teaching that men and women could live above all sin." What does she mean by this? After all, she herself frequently asserts that living without sin is a possibility, so why should she fault someone else who says the same thing? Here are a few examples of what she says in this regard:

[Christ's] life is an example of what our lives may be. [48]

Christ came in the form of humanity, and by His perfect obedience He proved that humanity and divinity combined can obey every one of God's precepts. [49]

Christ took humanity and bore the hatred of the world that He might show men and women that they could live without sin, that their words, their actions, their spirit, might be sanctified to

---

48 *Selected Messages*, Book Two, 253

49 *Christ's Object Lessons*, 314

God. We can be perfect Christians if we will manifest this power in our lives. [50]

To every one who surrenders fully to God is given the privilege of living without sin, in obedience to the law of heaven. [51]

In His life He has given us a representation of what repentant sinners may become. He was pure and undefiled. From His lips escaped no word that could leave a stain upon His character. All through the Scriptures He has given us assurances that through His grace we may attain the same perfection of character that He attained. [52]

Many more such statements might be quoted, of course, but this is surely enough. The final quotation is perhaps of particular interest, since it was published in 1903, right in the middle of the pantheism crisis.

But all this makes it look like Ellen White is contradicting herself, or at least faulting others for saying the same thing she said. What did she mean when she spoke of "theories teaching that men and women could live above all sin." The statement itself gives the answer when it tells us that the man in question accepted these theories and as a result he "left his wife and children and went to live with another woman."

This particular "living above all sin" of which she wrote was clearly the variety that attempts to do so by negating the law, rather than by reforming the life. It's all wrong, of course, but nothing new:

When [the Apostle John] came in contact with those who were breaking the law of God, yet claiming that they were living without sin, he did not hesitate to warn them of their fearful deception. [53]

Perhaps the most useful lesson from this consideration of the Alpha's similarity to the heresies of earlier years is to recognize the broader scope of Ellen White's comments. When she says "pantheism," she may not necessarily be speaking as specifically as the dictionary definition of the word might lead us to expect.

---

50   *Mind, Character, and Personality*, vol. 2, 527

51   *Review and Herald*, September 27, 1906

52   *Signs of the Times*, June 10, 1903

53   *Acts of the Apostles*, 554

Another point to consider from this comparison is the emphasis on "free-lovism." The connection seems to be that when the human mind and heart is cut loose from the restraining influence of God's law, fueled by some deceptive teaching that makes it seem just fine to do as one pleases, then it should be no surprise that sensuality is one of the most common results. Perhaps there is a close relationship between the final, "Omega" deception, and other comments foretelling temptations to licentiousness at the end of time:

> The crime that brought the judgments of God upon Israel was that of licentiousness. The forwardness of women to entrap souls did not end at Baal-peor. … Israel would have bravely met their enemies in battle, and resisted them, and come off conquerors; but when women invited their attention and sought their company and beguiled them by their charms, they did not resist temptations. They were invited to idolatrous feasts, and their indulgence in wine further beclouded their dazed minds. … Those who had never flinched in battle, who were brave men, did not barricade their souls to resist temptation to indulge their basest passions. …
>
> Near the close of this earth's history Satan will work with all his powers in the same manner and with the same temptations wherewith he tempted ancient Israel just before their entering the land of promise. He will lay snares for those who claim to keep the commandments of God, and who are almost on the borders of the heavenly Canaan. … He is not aiming especially at the lower and less important marks, but. … men in responsible positions… over such he sets his hellish powers and his agencies at work. … If he be a messenger of righteousness, and has had great light, or if the Lord has used him as his special worker in the cause of truth, then how great is the triumph of Satan! How he exults! How God is dishonored![54]

There is value in noting the degree of concern which all this pantheism business caused Ellen White. We've read her comments, and it's obvious she felt strongly about the subject, but how did that play out in practical life? We know she wrote letters, had private

---

54   *Review and Herald*, May 17, 1887

conversations, and gave public sermons on the topic... but she was in a unique situation. No one else was the messenger of the Lord. What about all the rest of the church members? What were they to do?

It turns out that her advice to others was mostly on things *not* to do. Refuse to get drawn into pointless discussions on the nature of God, for one. But the most notable advice—and the one which caused the greatest impact—was aimed at what we today might consider the college-aged or young adult segment of the church (and their parents, of course).

> I was shown that efforts would be made to call our leading men [to Battle Creek] to investigate the Scriptures, and discuss points of difference. I was then instructed that the students who had been called to Battle Creek, and the ministers held there, are in a dangerous atmosphere. [55]

> Some think it strange that I write, "Do not send your children to Battle Creek." I was instructed in regard to the danger of the worldly influence in Battle Creek. I have written hundreds of pages regarding the danger of having so large a sanitarium, and of calling so many people together in one place. The young people in Battle Creek are in danger. They will come in contact with error. Years ago I did not think that they would meet these errors right in the sanitarium; but when *Living Temple* came out, and some of our ministers told me that there was in it nothing but what I had been teaching all my life, I saw how great the danger was. I saw that blindness had fallen upon some who had long known the truth. [56]

> There are many things that I have not wanted to specify, but I am compelled to do this by the course that Dr. Kellogg takes. The last move made—the sending out of *Living Temple*—is a sample of the working of the man's mind. He makes the statement that he cannot see in *Living Temple* the things that I have said are there. Why can he not see them? Because his mind is

---

55   *Special Testimonies*, Series B, No. 2, 36

56   *Sermons and Talks*, vol. 1, 343

being worked by the very one who seduced the angels of God in the heavenly courts.

The efforts that Dr. Kellogg makes to call the youth to Battle Creek, notwithstanding the plain testimonies that have been given, show that he is working under the advice of the one who talked with Eve. Through this subtle reasoning the future of the cause is imperiled. I shall now have to be far more explicit than I have been in the past. I shall be compelled to make statements that I have not wanted to make, but I must be more explicit in order to save the flock of God from deceptive influences. [57]

Those who are carrying on the work of our sanitariums are not to shun responsibility and neglect their duty in order to give Dr. Kellogg the right of way. He has drawn many of our youth to Battle Creek, and they have become fastened where they will be brought under influences opposed to God. They are not to be kept under this training. Cut loose, cut loose, is my message. Souls are being deceived; sentiments are being received which originate with satanic agencies. Cut loose, cut loose. [58]

Perhaps the most foundational element of this warning against such influences is that it was unsafe to deal with them because people weren't smart enough, or righteous enough, or sufficiently connected with God to detect and resist them. It was a simple idea, but one which struck directly at human self-confidence. Our culture is not accustomed to being told that we aren't up to a challenge of this nature. The issue thus became a test of faith. Were the members and the leaders of God's church willing to acknowledge His wisdom in this and take the warning, or were they going to trust their own intelligence to figure it all out for ourselves?

That was the "Alpha"; will there be parallels in the "Omega"?

---

57   *Manuscript Releases*, vol. 13, 378

58   *Manuscript Releases*, vol. 21, 175

Chapter Six
He Said, She Said

WE have seen reference several times to the one aspect of the whole pantheism issue that most stung Ellen White. It was one thing (and a bad enough thing, at that) for someone to be teaching heresy; but when it was claimed that it all echoed Ellen White's own writings, that really hurt!

When she describes this development, she seems totally dumbfounded. You get a mental picture of her standing with eyes wide in amazement and chin hanging down in shock. How could Dr. Kellogg say such a thing! And how could *anyone* believe it when he did?

Sadly, there were quite a few who convinced themselves Kellogg's version of things was more believable than Ellen White's. There was little she could do but register her protest. But Kellogg had his problems, too. Despite the size and luxury of the new sanitarium building (or, really, *because* of the size and luxury of the new sanitarium building) the doctor was certainly not flush with cash. We've already noted Dr. Edwards' comment about the bonds he was trying to sell, and Ellen White's opposition to them. [59]

The simple reality was that, with the greatest proportion of the rank and file members of the church, Ellen White still had influence. That's why Kellogg's bonds weren't selling, and why there were fewer young people going to Battle Creek. Her comments and influence were taking time to filter down through the denominational grape vine, but it was doing so clearly enough to impact Kellogg's plans. What could he do?

For a time, at least, Dr. Kellogg and his associates felt they could get away with saying that *The Living Temple* really *was* in harmony with Ellen White's writings—she just didn't quite understand it yet. There is little doubt that some of the people involved actually believed this. On the strength of that argument, Kellogg's first printing of three thousand copies went out. It was one of those "It's easier to

---

59   See page 12

ask forgiveness later than to get permission now" sort of things. It seems that some people, at least, may have really hoped to convince Ellen White that it was a good thing.

To put it mildly, that effort was doomed; Ellen White wasn't accepting that idea *at all*. Even if no one else understood what she had written, she did—and it *wasn't* the same as *The Living Temple*. Before long, letter after letter and article after article was going out to set the record straight.

> I am compelled to speak in denial of the claim that the teachings of *Living Temple* can be sustained by statements from my writings. There may be in this book expressions and sentiments that are in harmony with my writings. And there may be in my writings many statements which, taken from their connection, and interpreted according to the mind of the writer of *Living Temple*, would seem to be in harmony with the teachings of this book. This may give apparent support to the assertion that the sentiments in *Living Temple* are in harmony with my writings. But God forbid that this sentiment should prevail.[60]

> The Lord has a controversy with those who make of no effect the testimonies of His Spirit. He is dishonored by those who reject the light given concerning *The Living Temple*, telling you [Dr. Kellogg] that you have been misjudged. The warnings given regarding this book should be received, believed, and acted upon.[61]

> My dear brother [Dr. David Paulson], you are making a great mistake. … Will you unite with Dr. Kellogg to make it appear that the Testimonies which God has given through his Holy Spirit, sustain these theories, which are being advanced only as a "feeler?" Unless a change of heart takes place, the errors already published will be followed by other misleading theories. …[62]

---

60 *Selected Messages*, Book One, 203

61 *Manuscript Releases*, vol. 11, 318

62 This comment almost makes it sound like Ellen White was a "conspiracy theorist." No doubt Dr. Kellogg would have rejected any such assertion, and perhaps sincerely

I hear that you are trying to make it appear that the sentiments expressed in *Living Temple* in regard to God can be sustained by my writings; therefore I am obliged to make a statement of denial of this, that our people shall not be deceived.[63]

Kellogg's next step was to admit that the book had a few technical problems… but not really enough to get worried about. Ellen White disagreed:

It is not safe to trust in Dr. Kellogg. I dare not do it. I have not written to him much, recently, but I may have to send something soon. I have not the least confidence in his present attitude toward many things. I learn that notwithstanding all I have written regarding *The Living Temple*, a book that was written under the inspiration of the arch-deceiver; notwithstanding the many plain messages that I have delivered in the *Review and Herald* and in letters to our brethren in responsibility, Dr. Kellogg now admits only a few of the mistakes he has made, and still supposes that in former years I taught the same errors. This reveals a blindness beyond conception. All that I can now do is to watch developments closely. I can not see that it would do the least particle of good to say more than I have said. [64]

The doctor's new position didn't last long either, for the simple reason that Ellen White wasn't cooperating at all. So the Kellogg team adjusted again. Now the idea was that they really did love and respect the Spirit of Prophecy, but that people needed to understand that there were *parts* of what Ellen White wrote that weren't inspired like the other parts. The "problem" with those "uninspired" parts was that they just sort of slipped into the testimony almost accidentally, because someone somewhere had shared an opinion with Ellen White that wasn't quite exactly correct. As one should suspect by now, Ellen White wasn't going to let this story take root, either.

---

so. He may not have known where all this was headed for the simple reason that there was another intelligence behind it all. We'll look at this idea more in the next chapter.

63   *Spalding and Magan Collection*, 333

64   *Battle Creek Letters*, 103

I have my work to do, to meet the misconceptions of those who suppose themselves able to say what is testimony from God and what is human production. If those who have done this work continue in this course, satanic agencies will choose for them. ...

Those who have helped souls to feel at liberty to specify what is of God in the Testimonies and what are the uninspired words of Sister White, will find that they were helping the devil in his work of deception. [65]

Those who have gone out of the way have in their darkness put their human ideas into operation, supposing that when testimonies were sent them from God to point out their mistakes and their dangers, they could set their unsanctified judgment to work against the Holy Spirit, saying of the part that reproved their course, "Somebody has told her," and of the part in which their wrong course of action was not referred to, "That is of the Lord." [66]

I fully believed that if you were an honest man, you would see the need of pursuing an entirely different course of action; that you would accept the light coming to you in the messages that had been given, and work out a thorough change in yourself.

But instead of taking a right position, when something came that did not harmonize with your views, you said, "Somebody has told her." Thus it has been when anything has come that cuts across your track.

But I hoped and hoped that you would change, until I was instructed that the words meant to encourage you to take the right stand were exerting the opposite influence on you. A condition of things has come about that has opened the door to the enemy. Old thoughts, which were never killed, have had

---

65   *Manuscript Releases*, vol. 4, 63

66   *Manuscript Releases*, vol. 21, 416

a resurrection, and the ideas set forth in *Living Temple* [are] the result.[67]

And through it all, Kellogg maintained that he was a firm believer in the Spirit of Prophecy. To us this may seem unbelievable. But with much slower communication in those days, even this line was good enough to gain him a little more time and money. But, as expected, Ellen White wasn't buying it.

Man's mind, although divinely created, may be worked by another power, as was the mind of Adam, a man who had walked and talked with God. ...

And thus it has been in the case of the one who has long stood at the head of our medical work. He often declares that he has always believed the messages God has given through Sister White; and yet he has done very much to undermine confidence in the validity of the testimonies. Many have accepted so fully his version of plain messages, that the testimonies have come to have no effect on them. As a result, not a few have gone into infidelity. O, how many he has influenced to view things as he has viewed them! How often he has led others to think, "Somebody has told Sister White"![68]

Letters have come to me with statements made by men who claimed to have asked Dr. Kellogg if he believes the testimonies that Sister White bears. He declares that he does, but he does not.[69]

That was the "Alpha"; will there be parallels in the "Omega"?

---

67   *Special Testimonies*, Series B, No. 7, 46–47

68   *Special Testimonies*, Series B, No. 7, 53

69   *Special Testimonies*, Series B, No. 7, 60

Chapter Seven
What Manner of Spirit?

A S the circumstances of the Alpha unfolded in the early 1900s, one aspect that must have seemed odd to many people was Ellen White's denunciation of pantheism. For starters, those who had gone to General Conference sessions while Ellen White was in Australia had gotten used to the occasional off-the-beaten-path comment from some of the common speakers. It doesn't seem likely that many of the "normal church members" were oohing and aahing over the air and water, but they had heard that sort of thing, and nobody had seemed concerned then.

As we saw back on page 29, Ellen White had expected the leaders of the church to spot pantheism as a problem and deal with it wisely. The fact that this hadn't happened was of great concern to her, and prompted her to make her public statements on the subject. [70]

There was probably a good amount of embarrassment at church headquarters over some of her comments on this failure. But mingled with that, there must have been some surprise when the leaders read that these quirky ideas that some of their colleagues had been talking about were actually spiritualism! [71]

Now, spiritualism was an old and well known foe. Years before, Moses Hull, a successful Adventist evangelist of the time, had presumptuously (and single-handedly) tangled with a whole group of spiritualists in a public debate, and had never recovered himself. But that was a spiritualism that Adventists knew well. Séances, floating tables, and spirits of the dead were clearly out of bounds. But this stuff about *life* and *water* and *air*. ... *This* is spiritualism?

---

70 See page 30

71 There is some danger of confusion because of two different meanings attached to the word "spiritualistic." Prior to the emergence of modern spiritism in the 1850s, it was common to use the word spiritualistic to mean "spiritual rather than material." Ellen White occasionally uses this meaning, and so it is important to be aware of this. Here is one such example: "These spiritualize the doctrines of present truth until there is no distinction between the substance and the shadow." *General Conference Bulletin,* April 6, 1903.

Yes, according to Ellen White:

There is a strain of spiritualism coming in among our people, and it will undermine the faith of those who give place to it, leading them to give heed to seducing spirits and doctrines of devils. [72]

But how can there be spiritualism without any involvement of the supposed spirits of the dead? Clearly, it doesn't work that way… unless "spiritualism" takes in something broader than we have commonly thought. When we consider the full range of Spirit of Prophecy counsel in the case of the Alpha, that's the only understanding that works.

At the heart of Christianity is the relationship of the believer to "the Word." Scripture's dual use of the expression to represent both Jesus and the instruction given in the Bible provides only the slimmest of bases for confusion. The apostle John speaks of Jesus as "the Word" five times. [73] No other Bible writer uses the term that way, and the context of John's statements makes it impossible to not understand his intention.

And yet it is this very issue to which Kellogg's pantheism was leading, the substitution of a subjectively experienced Word (the indefinable "essence" of Christ) for the objectively defined instruction of the written Word of God. This reliance on a subjective supernatural experience is readily seen in all "mystical" religious experiences, whether it be in the context of Hinduism, Buddhism, Animism, Catholicism, Judaism, Islam, or blatant Spiritualism. Each of these religious traditions has a well developed mystical element which is easily at home with the mystics from any of the others. Though the "spiritual entity" may vary (an eagle for the animist, say; Shiva for the Hindu; the Virgin Mary for the Catholic; Aunt Matilda for the spiritist; or a "spirit guide" for the New Ager), mysticism always leads sooner or later to the establishment of a subjective controlling element that draws its influence from the overwhelming impact of the supernatural encounter experienced by the mystic.

Notice Ellen White's comment:

---

72   *Manuscript Releases*, vol. 21, 173

73   John 1:1, 14; 1 John 1:1, 5:7, and Revelation 19:13

Let the world go into spiritualism, into theosophy, into pantheism, if they choose. We are to have nothing to do with this deceptive branch of Satan's work. The pleasing sentiments of pantheism will lead many souls into forbidden paths. [74]

Notice the list—spiritualism, theosophy, pantheism—and then notice how the next sentence refers to these three: "*this* deceptive branch." What to many might appear as separate and distinct "spiritual belief systems" are in actual fact united at the heart by the common element of mysticism, the opening of the mind to direct demonic influence.

We need not the mysticism that is in this book [*The Living Temple*]. Those who entertain these sophistries will soon find themselves in a position where the enemy can talk with them, and lead them away from God. [75]

The mysticism of Kellogg's rather watered down pantheism was a far cry from the full package as might be seen in any of its more developed forms. But mysticism is at its very heart opposed to the means of communication that God has chosen. It's the equivalent of a country's military gaining full control of their enemy's command and control channels. Then, in fact, the enemy *can* "talk with them, and lead them away from God."

Think of it like this: the Allied forces are halfway across the English Channel on D-Day when a high-priority, secure communication comes direct from General Eisenhower, the Supreme Allied Commander. The command is simple—"Abort Operation Overlord; turn back." Well, it didn't happen that way, it's true. But if you were Adolph Hitler and could have made it happen… wouldn't you have *wanted* it to happen?

In any military conflict, short of outright victory the highest of all prizes is taking over the enemy's communications. Don't you think the devil is smart enough to know this? Of course, if you can't take control of the enemy's communication channel, the next best thing is to disrupt it or cut it off entirely.

---

74   *Special Testimonies*, Series B, No. 6, 43

75   *Review and Herald*, October 22, 1903

Those accepting the theories regarding God that are introduced in *Living Temple* are in great danger of being led finally to look upon the whole Bible as a fiction; for these theories make of no effect the plain word of God. [76]

Ellen White makes it clear that, sadly, all this came to pass in Dr. Kellogg's experience:

When you wrote that book [*Living Temple*] you were not under the inspiration of God. There was by your side the one who inspired Adam to look at God in a false light. Your whole heart needs to be changed, thoroughly and entirely cleansed. [77]

No greater deception could be presented to the minds of men than the representation you have made of God in the pleasing fables you have advocated. Souls will be lost through the sowing of the sentiments found in *Living Temple*. In presenting error you have united with the prince of darkness in his work of seducing souls to eternal ruin.[78]

At the time of the [1903] General Conference in Oakland, I was forbidden by the Lord to have any conversation with Dr. Kellogg. During that meeting a scene was presented to me, representing evil angels conversing with the Doctor, and imbuing him with their spirit, so that at times he would say and do things, the nature of which he could not understand. He seemed powerless to escape from the snare. At other times he would appear to be rational.[79]

At the Oakland General Conference I could not explain fully why I was to have no conversation with Dr. Kellogg. It was because Satanic agencies were communicating with him, and much that I might have said would have been misstated and

---

76   *Special Testimonies*, Series B, No. 7, 38

77   *Manuscript Releases*, vol. 11, 314

78   *Manuscript Releases*, vol. 11, 251

79   *Battle Creek Letters*, 101

misinterpreted. This is also the reason why, for a time, I could not send letters direct to him.[80]

As sad as the doctor's course may be, though, there is nothing that can be done about it now. He and all the others in this story are long dead, and their cases are in the hands of the Lord to judge. What matters now is what we can learn from their experience and the instruction given us concerning it, for we are told that what has been in the past is to come upon God's church again.

> Scientific, spiritualistic sentiments, representing the Creator as an essence pervading all nature, have been given to our people, and have been received even by some who have had a long experience as teachers in the word of God. The results of this insidious devising will break out again and again. [81]

> Satan, clothed in the garb of an angel of light, presents for the study of the human mind subjects which seem very interesting, and which are full of scientific mystery. In the investigation of these subjects, men are led to accept erroneous conclusions, and to unite with seducing spirits in the work of propounding new theories which lead away from the truth.

> There is danger that the false sentiments expressed in the books that they have been reading will sometimes be interwoven by our ministers, teachers, and editors with their arguments, discourses, and publications, under the belief that they are the same in principle as the teachings of the Spirit of truth. The book *Living Temple* is an illustration of this work, the writer of which declared in its support that its teachings were the same as those found in the writings of Mrs. White. Again and again we shall be called to meet the influence of men who are studying sciences of satanic origin, through which Satan is working to make a nonentity of God and of Christ. [82]

---

80 *Battle Creek Letters*, 104

81 *Special Testimonies*, Series B, No. 7, 36

82 *Review and Herald*, August 6, 1908

If we are to be called "again and again" to meet such influences, it seems only wise to expect that such a test may indeed come to us as individuals and as a church. This is the reason for this book: to look at the past, to gain from the instruction given, and to apply it to the events and circumstances of our own day. We are not given every detail, of course, but many general principles, and the occasional more specific piece of counsel. Many quotations which might fit into this category to some degree have already been cited, but there are a few more specific details that deserve careful consideration in this connection.

In His Word the Lord declared what He would do for Israel if they would obey His voice. But the leaders of the people yielded to the temptations of Satan, and God could not give them the blessings He designed them to have, because they did not obey His voice but listened to the voice and policy of Lucifer. This experience will be repeated in the last years of the history of the people of God, who have been established by His grace and power. Men whom He has greatly honored will in the closing scenes of this earth's history pattern after ancient Israel. ...

Bear this in mind. History is being repeated. The perils that God's people encountered in past ages, they will encounter again, intensified. Satan has obtained influence over men whom God has honored above all human intelligence, as He honored Solomon. [83]

If Dr. Kellogg would stand solidly with his ministering brethren, they could help him, and he could help them. But he has started on a track which, if followed, will lead to the tearing down of the foundation upon which our faith is based. Spiritualistic sentiments have been presented in so plausible a manner that

---

[83] *Manuscript Releases*, vol. 13, 379–380. In context, this seems to primarily refer to Kellogg, though Ellen White's use of the plural "men" opens the door to a wider application.

Still, the reference to "men whom God has honored above all human intelligence" would seem to have primary reference to Dr. Kellogg. Ellen White often said that the Lord had blessed Kellogg with skill and understanding that was intended to be used as a blessing to God's work.

our medical missionary workers have been fascinated by them. I pray that they will not continue to foster these ideas. Their work now is to put away from them these pleasing fables.

My brother, I cannot understand how you could tell me that there is in The *Living Temple* nothing that is not in harmony with what we as a people believe. I thought you a true watch-man, quick to see when evil from the enemy was stealing into our ranks. I thought you would be wide-awake to discern the approach of the enemy, and give the alarm. The rebuke of God rests upon you because you did not discern the dangerous character of the fables that were being circulated. The rebuke of God is upon every minister and every medical missionary leader who has been asleep on the walls of Zion, when as vig-ilant watchmen they should have warned the people of the Lord against the dangers threatening them.

Wonderful scenes, with which Satan will be closely connected, will soon take place. God's Word declares that Satan will work miracles. He will make people sick, and then will suddenly re-move from them his satanic power. They will then be regard-ed as healed. These works of apparent healing will bring Sev-enth-day Adventists to the test. Many who have had great light will fail to walk in the light, because they have not become one with Christ. His instruction is not palatable to them. [84]

A final consideration of the spirit of the Alpha apostasy may be in order here, but this time by way of contrast. Perhaps you have noticed, throughout these quotations from Ellen White, that she carried a continual burden on her heart for Dr. Kellogg's soul. The selections quoted here have focused on her counsel concerning his apostasy, and so the notes of concern, the expressions of encourage-ment, and the invitations to accept the Lord's will, have appeared here only coincidentally.

But to ignore this element would terribly distort the work of God's servant, for it easily comprises the larger portion of most ev-ery original source that has been cited. To fully represent this aspect

---

84   *Manuscript Releases*, vol. 19, 358

of Ellen White's effort is not possible in the space available, but a few representative examples simply must be included:

> Dr. Kellogg, you may tell me that you do not believe the messages I send you, but I know that this is not true. You know of the experience that God has given me in His work. You can not deny that He has led and sustained me. You may close your eyes and ears to the messages that God sends, but after all, you do believe them. And you may depend on this: a mother could not hold more firmly to a child that she dearly loves than I shall hold to you. I expect to see you engaged in the work that God has given you, and I pray for you constantly, in private prayer and at family worship. Sometimes I am awakened in the night, and rising I walk the room, praying, "O Lord, hold Dr. Kellogg fast. Do not let him go. Keep him steadfast. Anoint his eyes with the heavenly eyesalve, that he may see all things clearly."[85]

> Last night, after going to rest, I wrestled in earnest prayer for you until eleven o'clock. Then I slept until three. I then rose and dressed, and continued my prayer that God would draw back the curtain and let you see where you stand. I have felt that it was of little use for me to write more to you, for the many letters that I have written do not seem to have that [effect? result?] which I so much hoped they would accomplish. And yet my burden does not leave me, because you cannot see yourself as God sees you. [86]

> This morning I received a letter from you. I would encourage you in the efforts that you are making to press into the light. We pray for you, that you will work out your own salvation with fear and trembling, knowing that it is God which worketh in you, both to will and to do of His good pleasure. I would not say one word to destroy hope. I know that the enemy will work diligently to dishearten right effort. [87]

---

85 *Battle Creek Letters*, 64

86 *Manuscript Releases*, vol. 11, 313

87 *Manuscript Releases*, vol. 11, 318

After bearing Testimonies of warning to Dr. Kellogg, I would weep as if my heart would break. Night after night, upon awaking, I would pray for him; I hoped and prayed that he would come out into the clear light. Thus the burden of his soul rested upon me after I returned from the Oakland General Conference. [88]

Just as valid as any lesson we might (and should) learn about the errors and dangers of the Alpha is the lesson taught by these quotations. Every soul is a soul to save. Sadly, it often seemed that Ellen White was nearly alone in her care for Dr. Kellogg. Indeed, we have a number of letters in which she urges others to work to save the doctor.

One of the more interesting examples of this is most fully told in the words of Dr. S.P.S. Edwards. The setting is the contentious General Conference session of 1903, just before "pantheism" became a major focus in the strife between Dr. Kellogg and the General Conference leadership.

I met Sarah [McEnterfer, Ellen White's assistant] in the P[acific] P[ress] Business office and she said that she and Mother [Ellen White] were taking the evening train to St. Helena, and she wanted Dr. and Mrs. Paulson and me and my wife to accompany her. We were to get on the train at Fruitvale [a few miles from Oakland], so no one would know we were going. We followed instructions and when we entered the car found very few passengers. We sat down across the isle from Sister White. She smiled and looked out of the window. Not a word was said until after we got off the train at St. Helena, then from Sarah a statement that Mother wished to see us at 10:00 the next morning at Elmshaven. We took the San. Bus to the Sanitarium in deep thought.

After being assigned to our rooms, doctor Paulson called me and said for me to find a quiet place where we could talk. We went out doors and up the hill until we found a secluded spot and then [he asked] simply two questions: "What? Why?" We got down and prayed and our answer was, "wait."

---

88 *Spalding and Magan Collection,* 335

The next morning we four walked down the hill to Elmshaven where Sarah was waiting. We were taken up to the study and Mother met us with a smile and after we were seated she started on a most interesting story about events in her life and our lives with which she was conversant. For an hour she entertained us, but not a word about "the message." Finally she turned to me and said:… "I love Dr. Kellogg. He may be lost. I hope and pray not. If he is lost, let him go with you brethren standing by with your hands on his shoulders trying to save him." She then sweetly dismissed us, and Doctor Paulson and I walked up the hill arm in arm: we had a mission and a commission. We tried to carry it out. We made some mistakes in our methods. Sister White reproved us. We tried again. I have her letters of reproof and correction. Very precious!…

The last time I met Doctor Kellogg, was at a dinner in the Loma Linda Sanitarium dining room. A group of us gathered around him. There was George Thomason, D.D. Comstock, Frank Abbott, Ben Colver, and myself, all doctor friends. We said in parting: "Are you not coming with us?" He answered after a minute of thought, "Perhaps I am nearer with you than you know." And so he was left with God, with our hands on his shoulders. [89]

The point of this story is obvious enough; Ellen White loved John Harvey Kellogg and wanted to see him saved. A minor sub-plot is interesting as well: the episode above took place immediately after the 1903 General Conference session, but a few months later, at the Autumn Council in Takoma Park, it was Dr. Paulson who supported Dr. Kellogg and argued with the General Conference president. You may remember the story of how Paulson "shook his finger at Daniells and declared: 'You are making the mistake of your life. After all this turmoil, some of these days you will wake up to find yourself rolled in the dust, and another will be leading the forces.'"

Did Ellen White make a mistake? Did she put the wrong man on the job? No. As Dr. Edwards said, "we made some mistakes." This was perhaps Paulson's most serious mistake, but letters from

---

[89] Sanford P.S. Edwards, *Memoirs of SDA Pioneers*, 13–14

Ellen White brought him around; he eventually recovered his spiritual bearings, and was a very productive worker for the Lord till his death. The point is simply this: it is our privilege and commission to work to save souls. All souls. Even those who are in great error and hurting God's church. No, not "even those"; it is "*especially* those."

> Scientific, spiritualistic sentiments, representing the Creator as an essence pervading all nature, have been given to our people, and have been received even by some who have had a long experience as teachers in the word of God. The results of this insidious devising will break out again and again. There are many for whom special efforts will have to be put forth to free them from this specious deception. [90]

That was the "Alpha"; will there be parallels in the "Omega"?

---

90 *Special Testimonies*, Series B, No. 7, 36

Chapter Eight
Fast Forward

MORE than a century has passed since Dr. Kellogg wrote The *Living Temple* and Ellen White warned us of the Omega apostasy to come. Over time, as one might expect, the details of the era have receded into history and the warning has faded from view. Through the years, different ones have called attention to the Omega prophecy, suggesting various events and issues as possible fulfillments. Regardless, time has gone on, silently testifying to the fact that none of the issues of the past have been the *final* apostasy to afflict God's church.

Yet the passage of time no more proves the prophecy false than it negates the promise of the Second Coming. In recent years, a new focus of concern has arisen. A relative few have marked its entrance into the church with consternation while some others have hailed it with joy; for many years, most were not aware of it at all, and when it was brought to their attention they have commonly ignored the matter because of unconcern or confusion.

Simply dismissing the question, however, is an option with a rapidly expiring shelf life. This does not appear to be a discussion that will go away if ignored, and so prominent voices have been raised, both for and against these practices. Perhaps most well known in this regard is the Sabbath sermon given on the third of July, 2010, by newly elected General Conference President, Elder Ted N.C. Wilson. He advised the church:

> Don't reach out to movements or megachurch centers outside the Seventh-day Adventist Church which promise you spiritual success based on faulty theology. Stay away from non-Biblical spiritual disciplines or methods of spiritual formation that are rooted in mysticism such as contemplative prayer, centering prayer, and the emerging church movement in which they are promoted. Look *within* the Seventh-day Adventist Church to humble pastors, evangelists, Biblical scholars, leaders, and

departmental directors who can provide evangelistic methods and programs that are based on solid Biblical principles and "The Great Controversy Theme."[91]

There have always been elements of non-Adventist Christianity which have been a concern to the church. There have always been ideas and teachings which have produced conflicting opinions among the leadership and laity alike. And yet to many observers, *these* issues seem different somehow. Above and beyond the many specific points of contention is the simple fact that these issues include many points akin to the Alpha apostasy of years ago.

Only time will tell, of course, if the Omega is now upon us. But with so much at stake, surely the question deserves careful and prayerful study. In this regard we may be thankful we live in what well known author Leonard Sweet has referred to as a "Google age." It is oddly fitting that, for this topic—with its focus on the "postmodern" world—the information involved is almost all readily available on the Internet, conveniently indexed and made searchable by modern technology. On this issue, Dr. Sweet is certainly correct.

---

91   scribd.com/doc/33861749/Ted-N-C-Wilson-Sermon-Go-Forward#download

Chapter Nine
What's This All About?

FOR anyone new to the topic, the terms "emerging church," "spiritual formation," "spiritual direction," and "contemplative prayer" may not mean much. We haven't space here to go into every detail of these movements, but a short introduction at least, will be helpful.

The emerging church (sometimes, *emergent* church) movement began with a focus on youth and young adults. These, so the thinking went, were to be the Christians who would "emerge" into the "postmodern" world. The term now covers many variations and ranges of practice, including worship styles, musical preference, and the general focus of the religious experience. These areas each deserve prayerful attention, for though changes in practice from age to age have certainly occurred, efforts to make these elements of Christian experience *more relevant* to each successive generation, run the risk of moving away from the principles of Scripture. Our primary interest in the emerging church movement, however, is the strong relationship between it and certain elements of our other terms—spiritual formation, spiritual direction, and contemplative prayer.

Spiritual formation is said to be the necessary means to *form* a fully developed Christian experience. The techniques most commonly included under this title were stipulated in 1548 by Ignatius Loyola, the founder of the Jesuit Order, but it is clear that he based his ideas on the teaching and experiences of Catholic mystics from centuries before. One such group commonly cited in this regard is the Desert Fathers of the ancient near east. For those unfamiliar with the Desert Fathers, a brief introduction from Wikipedia may be helpful. This online resource of choice for the postmodern generation tells us that the Desert Fathers—

> ... were Christian hermits, ascetics, and monks who lived mainly in the Scetes desert of Egypt beginning around the third century A.D. ... The most well known was Anthony the Great, who

moved to the desert in 270–271 and became known as both the father and founder of desert monasticism. … The Desert Fathers had a major influence on the development of [Roman Catholic] Christianity.

The desert monastic communities that grew out of the informal gathering of hermit monks became the model for Christian monasticism. The eastern monastic tradition at Mt. Athos and the western Rule of St. Benedict both were strongly influenced by the traditions that began in the desert. All of the monastic revivals of the Middle Ages looked to the desert for inspiration and guidance. [92]

Another term closely associated with spiritual formation is "spiritual direction." There are widely varying definitions of the term, which tends to make intelligent discussion difficult since two people may not mean the same thing when using the same words. More confusing yet is the tendency of some to profess that they mean only the most mild concepts associated with the term, while their actual practice may be far more akin to the radical end of the spectrum.

Here is an example of a fairly authoritative definition that frankly acknowledges the more extreme aspects that raise concern:

Spiritual direction is the contemplative practice of helping another person or group to awaken to the mystery called God in all of life, and to respond to that discovery in a growing relationship of freedom and commitment. —James Keegan, SJ, Roman Catholic, USA, on behalf of the 2005 Coordinating Council of Spiritual Directors International. [93]

Contemplative prayer (or *centering* prayer) is the core aspect of concern with each of the previous two movements. Though specific techniques vary in practice—from *lectio divina*, (repeating a word or sound over and over until it becomes meaningless and the mind shuts down), to the passivity of labyrinth walking, to various forms of mental relaxation through a focus on one's own breath or on a

---

92 en.wikipedia.org/wiki/Desert_Fathers

93 sdiworld.org/find-a-spiritual-director/what-is-spiritual-direction

visualized mental image—the most significant element is emptying the mind in search of spiritual enlightenment.

The subjective experience which comes through this kind of meditation can be extremely powerful, sometimes dramatically changing the course of the life—and with it, of course, the theology. It is the lure of this experience which has fueled meditative movements within many different belief systems over the centuries.

One well known author who has dealt with this topic is Daniel Goleman. In his book, *The Meditative Mind*, he wrote:

> The meditative practices and rules for living of these earliest Christian monks bear strong similarity to those of their Hindu and Buddhist renunciate brethren several kingdoms to the east. ... The meditative techniques they adopted for finding their God suggest either a borrowing from the East or a spontaneous recovery. [94]

"Recovery" is an interesting choice of wording. One might have expected him to say "discovery," but it would seem that this author feels that the "techniques" belonged first to some previous time or culture.

In an online review of Goleman's book, a "Buddhist practitioner and teacher" named Bodhipaksa provides an interesting summary that speaks directly to the point of concern with contemplative practices:

> Part Two of the book offers an overview of a number of meditative traditions: Hindu Bakti meditation, Jewish meditation, Christian meditation, Sufism, Patanjali's Yoga tradition, Tantra, Tibetan Buddhism, and Zen. For me this was the most fascinating part of the book. In fact I'd go as far as to say it's one of the most eye-opening spiritual documents I've read.

> The commonalities between the various traditions are immense, and I came away with a deep respect for non-Buddhist traditions. It's clear that within Christianity, Judaism, Islam, etc., there have been deep currents of meditative experience, and

---

94 Daniel Goleman, *The Meditative Mind* (Los Angeles, CA: Tarcher/Putnam, Inc., 1988), 53

correspondingly deep insights. I'm convinced now that there have been enlightened practitioners in many traditions besides Buddhism—something I hadn't really contemplated before. I still consider other traditions to be hampered by their theological baggage, however, and for that reason I do still consider the Buddha's insight to have gone further than others', but I am still humbled and reverential toward the Desert Fathers and other non-Buddhist meditators. [95]

It's possible, of course, to consider this similarity of practice from two different points of view. If the experience is of God, then we should rejoice that so many who know little or nothing of the gospel could be blessed by this contact with the Lord. If these supernatural encounters are *not* of God, however, the fact that so many from so many religions have had—and continue to have—such similar experiences is cause for real alarm.

The modern resurgence of spiritual formation is often traced to the writings of Thomas Merton, a Trappist monk who promoted "interfaith understanding." In practice, this meant incorporating the methods of Zen Buddhism, Taoism, Hinduism, Jainism, and Sufism into the contemplative practices of his Catholic Cistercian order. Merton wrote more than seventy books, many of which promoted this approach. [96]

William Meninger, another Trappist monk at St. Joseph's Abbey in Spencer, Massachusetts, had read Merton's works, and was seeking for a way to interact with those of other faiths. In 1974 he found an old copy of *The Cloud of Unknowing*, a book written by an English hermit in the 1300s. Like most mystical writings, this volume emphasized what is now known as contemplative prayer. Meninger began experimenting with the ideas, and teaching them to the younger monks of the abbey. He arranged for Hindu and Buddhist teachers

---

95 wildmind.org/blogs/book-reviews/the-meditative-mind-by-daniel-goleman

96 One classic example of Merton's thinking is the following: "It is a glorious destiny to be a member of the human race,… now [that] I realize what we all are. … If only they [people] could all see themselves as they really are… I suppose the big problem would be that we would fall down and worship each other. … At the center of our being is a point of nothingness which is untouched by sin and by illusions, a point of pure truth. … This little point… is the pure glory of God in us. It is in everybody." — *Conjectures of a Guilty Bystander*, 1989 edition, 157–158

to share their perspectives on spirituality, and when the classes were opened to the public they became quite popular.

In 1978, Richard Foster, a Quaker, wrote *The Celebration of Discipline*, which covers much the same ground. The book sold over a million copies and was ranked by *Christianity Today* as number three on their list of "best 100 books of the twentieth century." [97]

The description of the book provided on the Barnes & Noble website gives a taste of its emphasis:

> Foster shows that it is only by and through these practices that the true path to spiritual growth can be found. [98]

"Only by and through these practices"? Really? That's quite a claim.

Another major player in the modern development of these ideas was Henri Nouwen. An ordained Catholic priest, college professor, [99] and author, Nouwen gained a large loyal following, including *two* organizations named for him. That's a little ironic for a Universalist, actually, but apparently such sentiments as the following made him quite popular:

> The God who dwells in our inner sanctuary is the same as the one who dwells in the inner sanctuary of each human being. [100]

> The quiet repetition of a single word can help us to descend with the mind into the heart. … This way of simple prayer… opens us to God's active presence. [101]

> Prayer is "soul work" because our souls are those sacred centers where all is one and God is with us in the most intimate way. [102]

---

97   goodreads.com/list/show/13084._Christianity_Today_Books_of_the_20th_Century

98   barnesandnoble.com/w/celebration-of-discipline-richard-j-foster/1100150936?ean=9780060628390&isbn=2580060628393

99   Catholic University of Nijmegen, University of Notre Dame, Catholic Theological Institute in Utrecht, Yale Divinity School, Pontifical North American College in Rome, and Harvard Divinity School.

100 Henri Nouwen, *Here and Now: Living in the Spirit*, 22

101 Henri Nouwen, *The Way of the Heart*, 81

102 Henri Nouwen, *Bread for the Journey: A Daybook of Wisdom and Faith*, January 15

It is in the heart of God… that we can come to the full realization of the unity of all that is. [103]

Of course, statements of this kind do not make up the whole of Nouwen's writing, and so it's *possible* that people who value his work really only value the "*good parts*" of his books. Possible. …

What clearly *isn't* possible is to recommend his books and then shield those who go to read them from all of these kinds of statements. This is why Ellen White so often wrote words like the following:

> I tell you in the name of the Lord God of Israel, that Satan is presenting his sophistries to ministers and medical workers, and if our people listen to these sophistries, they will become impregnated with the same false idea of a popular religion that will cause them to develop into gods, and there will be no place in their lives for God or for Christ. [104]

> Suffer not yourselves to open the lids of a book that is questionable. There is a hellish fascination in the literature of Satan. It is the powerful battery by which he tears down a simple religious faith. Never feel that you are strong enough to read infidel books; for they contain a poison like that of asps. They can do you no good, and will assuredly do you harm. In reading them, you are inhaling the miasmas of hell. [105]

> Many think that in order to obtain an education it is necessary to study the productions of writers who teach infidelity, because their works contain some bright gems of thought. But who was the originator of these gems of thought? It was God, and God alone. He is the source of all light. Why should we wade through the mass of error contained in the works of pagans and infidels, for the sake of a few intellectual truths, when all truth is at our command?

> There is a reason why these men sometimes display remarkable wisdom. Satan himself was educated in the heavenly courts,

---

103 Henri Nouwen, *Bread for the Journey: A Daybook of Wisdom and Faith*, November 16

104 *Manuscript Releases*, vol. 10, 163

105 *Fundamentals of Christian Education*, 93

and he has a knowledge of good as well as of evil. He mingles the precious with the vile, and this is what gives him power to deceive. But because Satan has robed himself in garments of heavenly brightness, shall we receive him as an angel of light? The tempter has his agents, educated according to his methods, inspired by his spirit, and adapted to his work. Shall we co-operate with them? Shall we receive the works of his agents as essential to the acquirement of an education? [106]

In light of this instruction from the Lord, is there not reason to be concerned over quotations such as the following appearing in Seventh-day Adventist publications?

The other day a faculty colleague shared with me a recent book by Henri Nouwen. She had been blessed. And because she shared, I too was blessed. But I was struck by her comment: "Nouwen writes lots of books," she said. "And they all say the same thing. But I read them all anyway because I find them so helpful."

The book in question was In the *Name of Jesus: Reflections on Christian Leadership*, but it apparently makes little difference.[107]

When Henri Nouwen died prematurely last year, pastors everywhere lost a kindred spirit.

Nouwen suggests three disciplines that may help us drink our own cup. I was surprised to discover how silence, speaking, and acting can become disciplines of grace. Read this small book of 111 pages and be blessed as you practice these disciplines for yourself.[108]

When I would read books by Henri Nouwen, who gave up a tenured Harvard professorship and successful career for a simpler life of spiritual pursuits, I would think that maybe I should

106 *Testimonies*, vol. 8, 306

107 Alden Thompson, NPUC *Gleaner*, March 15, 1993, 6

108 Steve Willsey, *Ministry*, June 1997, 30–31; ministrymagazine.org/archives/1997/MIN1997-06.pdf

leave the hectic life of ministerial administrative activism. Maybe I should sign up for an overseas mission experience where I could work in a leper colony. ...

I would recommend most any of Henri Nouwen's books. Though a bit mystical, they do cause one to think about one's spiritual commitment. Another author that is inspiring is Eugene Peterson, particularly *Under the Unpredictable Plant* and *Working the Angles*.[109]

How safe is this? "The books are a bit mystical, but I don't suppose it's enough to hurt anyone. Go ahead and buy them." Really? In light of this next statement?

Just as long as men consent to listen to these sophistries, a subtle influence will weave the fine threads of these seductive theories into their minds, and men who should turn away from the first sound of such teaching will learn to love it. As loyal subjects we must refuse even to listen to these sophistries. Their influence is something like a deadly viper, poisoning the minds of all who listen. It is a branch of hypnotism, deadening the sensibilities of the soul."[110]

The last two quotations about Henri Nouwen, while from the same article, are spread apart. The first appears on page ten of the magazine, and the second is on page thirteen. Interestingly, on page twelve there is a large "pull quote" to break up the monotony of the text. It says:

There is a false spirituality in the world today that reflects more New Age mysticism than Biblical spirituality. We need to go to the Scriptures and find what is at the core of the spiritual life.[111]

---

109 Gordon Bietz, *Ministry*, December 1997, 10–13; ministrymagazine.org/archives/1997/MIN1997-12.pdf

110 *Manuscript Releases*, vol. 10, 163

111 Gordon Bietz, *Ministry*, December 1997, 12; ministrymagazine.org/archives/1997/MIN1997-12.pdf

That seems more than a little contradictory, does it not? Someone simply scanning through the paper would likely assume that the article was cautionary in nature, while the text itself recommends "most any of Henri Nouwen's books." But in the world of Henri Nouwen, this is not the only confusion. Here is a description of a one-day retreat featuring his lifework and teaching:

> Nouwen believes that there is true presence in absence and a necessary absence in presence as we journey together with others. In this retreat, we hope to learn how best to discern just when to be present and when to be absent and strike a healthy balance in the crucial interplay between presence and absence.[112]

What does any of that mean? The uninitiated won't have a clue, but some understand, and others will want to understand—thus setting up a desire and an openness to expose themselves to whatever the presentation happens to contain. And whether packaged one way or another, the contemplative element is sure to be there.

It is this concern with all forms of mysticism, of opening the mind to direct influence by demonic spirits, which lies at the base of the many cautions expressed by Seventh-day Adventists as they have witnessed these practices gaining acceptance among God's remnant people. Of particular concern in this regard is the rapid growth of a relatively new entity within the church. It is known as the One Project.

---

112 web.archive.org/web/20140615222102/https://e-giving.org/registration_v2.5/
      ViewEvent.asp?evntID=7092

Chapter Ten
The One Project

THE One Project is a relatively new actor on the Adventist stage. For those unfamiliar with the organization, a little background is in order. Conveniently enough, a succinct account of the program's beginnings is available from Andrews University.

Seven men shared a common bond: A deep love for Jesus. Their lives were already committed to Christ, but there was something in each of them that desired to be re-centered both in their own spiritual lives and within the Church they love. The question was: how?

Each of them are [sic] leaders in the Seventh-day Adventist Church: Alex Bryan, senior pastor at the Walla Walla University Church; Japhet De Oliveira, director of the Center for Youth Evangelism and for missions at Andrews University; Dany Hernandez, pastor for collegiate and young adult ministries at Forest Lake Adventist Church; Eddie Hypolite, associate youth director for the South England Conference, UK; Sam Leonor, pastor for La Sierra University; Tim Gillespie, pastor for young adult ministries at Loma Linda University Church of Seventh-day Adventists; and Terry Swenson, campus chaplain for Loma Linda University.

For nine months, they planned. Then came a day in July 2010 when five of them gathered at a Holiday Inn in Denver, joined periodically by the other two through the wonders of modern technology. For two days, they prayed. They fasted. They shared in communion. They reflected upon a simple statement: Jesus. All. …

As their conversations unfolded, their mission began to take shape. "What if we gathered together leaders from all over the world to celebrate the supremacy of Jesus in the Seventh-day Adventist Church?" "What if we gathered and focused on what it would mean for us, on a personal, and then local, and finally global community?" "What if we had honest conversation about our legacy, heritage and call for our Church today?" "What if we brought leaders, youth and adults, young and old, employed and retired, pastors and members and simply soaked in Jesus again?"

After two days together, the seven returned to their homes and ministries. And like a single pebble thrown into a still lake, creating circles that continue to widen, their renewed passion for Jesus in our Seventh-day Adventist Church spread. Their movement adopted the moniker the One project. ...

It began with seven. It has taken a grassroots hold upon a rapidly growing number of faithful believers in the Seventh-day Adventist Church. Their energy will undoubtedly spread. But that's exactly what those seven spiritual leaders dreamed of. [113]

And spread it did. Since that simple beginning in 2010, the One Project has held twelve major "gatherings" [114] in the United States, Europe, and Australia. The call for an emphasis on Jesus has resonated with many. It is, after all, pointless to try defending a Christianity without Christ. Judging from the list of "partners" on the project's website, [115] the idea of a renewed emphasis on Jesus has wide appeal.

---

113 andrews.edu/news/2011/03/one_project.html

114 The use of the term "gathering" is one of the many hallmarks of the emergent church movement which has come over into these kinds of organizations and activities within the Adventist Church. Try googling *emergent gatherings* to see what comes up.

115 The list of partners is separated into Platinum, Gold, Silver, and Bronze levels, and for each level is listed the commitments of the partnering organization and the One Project. All levels include the understanding that the partner "Will promote the One Project in their network."

Platinum: La Sierra University, Loma Linda University Campus Ministry, Walla Walla University Campus Ministry, Walla Walla University Church

Gold: Adventist Chaplaincy Ministries, Andrews University, Andrews University Campus Ministry, Australian Union Conference Youth Department, Fowler Films, La Sierra University Campus Ministry, North American Division, One Place

A quick look at the1project.org helps explain the organization's remarkable growth in "presence" among the young adults of the denomination. In 2010, five of the seven original founders held influential positions on Adventist university campuses. The trend is continued with the current board of eleven members. Included in that number are seven college and university staff, an assistant to the president of the North American Division, and a representative of the Hope Channel.[116] Needless to say, the One Project is well-positioned to exert a powerful influence on the church, and especially on its young adults.

The focus of the One Project is both simple and profound. As they themselves word it, it is:

Jesus. All.

This is in keeping with their goals and intent, and has the advantage of being an admirably catchy slogan. But it does raise questions.

Silver: British Union Conference, Danish Union of Churches, South England Conference, Union College Humanities Department

Bronze: AdventSource, Adventist Mission, Adventist University of Health Sciences, Andrews University Theological Seminary, Arizona Conference, Avondale College, Center for Creative Ministry, Center for Secular and Postmodern Studies, Finnish Union Conference, Florida Hospital Church, Florida Hospital College of Health Sciences, General Conference Youth and Young Adult Department, Greater Sydney Conference, Hope Channel, Illinois Conference, Inter-European Division Youth Department, John Hancock Center, Kellyville Church, Lake Union Conference, Life Source Adventist Fellowship, Mid-America Union, North American Division Youth and Young Adult Department, Netherlands Union Youth Department, Newbold College, North New South Wales Conference Youth Department, North Rhine-Westphalia German Conference, Ohio Conference, Pacific Press, Review and Herald, RE:LIVE Ministry, Submerge, South Pacific Division Youth Department, Union College, Union College Campus Ministries, Union College Religion Department, Washington Conference, Walla Walla University, ADRA Australia

the1project.org/about/partners

116 Alex Bryan (One Project Chair), senior pastor of the Walla Walla University Church; Japhet De Oliveira (One Project Chair), Senior Pastor for Boulder Seventh-day Adventist Church; Dilys Brooks, Associate Campus Chaplain, Loma Linda University; Ken Denslow (Ex Officio), Assistant to the President, North American Division; Lisa Clark Diller, History Dept. Chair, Southern Adventist University; David Franklin, Co-host of *Let's Pray!*, Hope Channel; Tim Gillespie, Faith Community and Health Liaison, Loma Linda University Health; Sam Leonor, University Chaplain, La Sierra University; Rod Long, Property Developer and Project Manager; Paddy McCoy, University Chaplain, Walla Walla University; Terry Swenson, University Chaplain, Loma Linda University; the1project.org/about/board

Perhaps the first and most obvious of these is, Does "Jesus. All." include "all of Jesus"? To disregard any portion of "the testimony of Jesus," for example, would seem to be a rather serious hole in the fabric of "Jesus. All."

But there are other questions as well:

> Yet, while "Jesus. All." sounds like a worthy motto—and it is in so many ways—the risk is trying to talk about Jesus without a context. Even God couldn't do that—thus, the incarnation, a particular expression of a real-person Jesus in a specific time, place, and culture. Neither can we follow Jesus without a context because it is only in a context that we function as disciples.
>
> A theologically or practically disembodied Jesus is simply a nice albeit amazing story—and risks a disembodied faith. Jesus in a bottle to be admired might still blow our minds and touch our hearts but might do little more. …
>
> As such, acontextual conversations about Jesus are unsustainable and soon become something less than promised. That's why, in a such a heavily Adventist setting as the One Project gatherings, the default context becomes the church, with a frustrating tendency to feel like a re-hashing of current church issues and past church grievances. [117]

As the writer above points out, context is important. In slightly different words, Ellen White said the same thing years ago.

> It is the relation that … ideas have to one another that gives them value. [118]

Inevitably the question would come up, "What is the relation of the One Project to the church?"

---

117 atoday.org/article/1322/opinion/z-archived-bloggers-columnists/ brown-nathan/2012/a-second-look-at-the-one-project

118 *Evangelism*, 648

Chapter Eleven

Relationships

GIVEN the admirable goal of the One Project to elevate Jesus in the Adventist Church, it seems a foregone conclusion that there was a perceived lack in this area. It wouldn't be the first time; a hundred and twenty-five years ago, the Spirit of Prophecy admonished us:

> As a people, we have preached the law until we are as dry as the hills of Gilboa that had neither dew nor rain. We must preach Christ in the law, and there will be sap and nourishment in the preaching that will be as food to the famishing flock of God. [119]

Not preaching Jesus is unquestionably a disaster, but context is everything. We are told to preach Christ *in* the law, not just Christ devoid of any setting. As might be imagined considering the reach and impact of the One Project, church members have wondered about its relationship to the work and theology of the church. And, considering the rapid growth of the movement, it has been natural to ask questions about its background. Unfortunately, these two issues raise some serious concerns.

The poignant account of the two days in the Denver motel is a great opening scene for the story of the One Project, but there is a background to it all that may be important as well. Though they are introduced to us simply as earnest church employees, it turns out that some of the group had known each other for years already. Tim Gillespie and Sam Leonor had been band mates, members of a moderately well known band called Big Face Grace. *The Adventist Review* describes them as "one of the first Adventist bands in the Christian rock arena."[120] *Adventist Today* says, "formed at Andrews University in the mid-90s, Big Face Grace has been featured on MTV's *Road*

---

119 *The Ellen G. White 1888 Materials*, 560

120 Adventist Review, May 5, 2005, 38; archives.adventistreview.org/issue_pdf. php?issue=2005-1518; registration required

Rules and ABC's *Making the Band* and played their Christian rock in stadiums for thousands. Four of the members are active pastors involved in college and youth ministries." [121]

> Michael [Knecht], Tim [Gillespie], Roy [Ice], and Sam [Leonor] all went to grad school together at a small university in southwest Michigan. They worked together on many different projects, but music was a priority to all of them. Michael had been asked to organize the music for a community event targeted toward teenagers. Michael played guitar, Tim sang, and Roy played the drums. The crowd went wild. The chemistry was incredible and the musical relationship continued. There were folk influences in the music, but the cohesiveness of the group soon yielded an eclectic yet distinct style.
>
> The newly formed band added Sam as bass player and Jason [Hutchinson], an undergrad at the University, as another guitarist. They quickly began booking gigs, however, had yet to decide on a name. The first name settled on was "the electric fishermen," which lasted about as long as their first concert. They quickly changed their name to "Big Face Grace" and it worked. The adventure had begun.
>
> BFG has now toured Australia, Finland, much of North America, and parts of Canada. They have thrilled audiences that ranged in attendance from 3 people to 11,000 and venues from barns to stadiums. [122]

For readers of an older generation it would be easy to pass over this musical relationship as a minor sidelight, but it is important to recognize the extent to which music forms a central element of young people's lives. To a large degree, music is now considered a primary mode of self-expression, something integrally related to one's identity and consequently to worship. We see the importance of this connection in this quotation from Tim Gillespie:

---

121 *Adventist Today*, Jan.–Feb. 2008, 21; atoday.org/issue_pdf.php?pdf=2008-01.pdf

122 delicatefade.com/biography.asp?ID=441

Worship is who we are. It is not defined by a song, a lyric, or an expression. It is the response to God and all his Glory. It is our mandate to call upon a God who is worthy of our praise. My first transition from [sic] Worship from a song service experience was at Willow Creek[123] at their leadership conference in 1994. Ever since I have been seeking to experience, teach, write, and create worship resources and experiences that resonate with others who are seeking the same truth in worship.[124]

Of course, reading a written description of anything musical falls several degrees short of reality. A live performance is clearly the best opportunity to understand such an experience, but lacking that, we may catch a sample of Big Face Grace through online video. Several of these may be found on YouTube.[125]

A second part of the One Project's back-story is hinted at in the brief biographies of the organization's board members as given on their website. It turns out that two of the five who met in that motel room (Alex Bryan and Terry Swenson) were classmates, having graduated together from the same university doctoral program in the spring of 2009.[126] Interestingly enough, a third member of the group (Tim Gillespie) would graduate from the same university, with the same degree, two years later, in the spring of 2011.[127] Even more surprising is that a *fourth* member of the group (Sam Leonor) is now pursuing a doctor's degree from the same university.[128]

Well, it has often been remarked that Adventism is a small world, so a coincidence like this might not be entirely unexpected at Andrews University, or Southern Adventist University, or Loma Linda University. But at George Fox University? That does seem strange… unless, perhaps there is something to be gained there that might have a particularly strong appeal to Seventh-day Adventists.

---

123 The role of Willow Creek in this experience is not irrelevant; this "megachurch" near Chicago has been one of the trendsetters in new methods of worship, and its pastor (Bill Hybels) is an acknowledged proponent of emerging church concepts.

124 adventpraise.org/article/65/artists/timothy-gillespie

125 See youtube.com/watch?v=s1ML2-V64_I, or youtube.com/watch?v=vhpI1Yj5iXY

126 the1project.org/person/details/1; the1project.org/person/details/11

127 the1project.org/person/details/8

128 the1project.org/person/details/9

A quick look at the background of the institution may be helpful, since relatively few Adventists would have reason to recognize the name. For starters, we note that the school is named for the founder of the Religious Society of Friends, commonly known as the Quakers. In broad outline, George Fox's religious views included the following points:

- Rituals can be safely ignored, as long as one experiences a true spiritual conversion.

- The qualification for ministry is given by the Holy Spirit, not by ecclesiastical study. This implies that anyone has the right to minister, assuming the Spirit guides them, including women and children. …

- [B]ecause God [is] within the faithful, believers [can] follow their own inner guide rather than rely on a strict reading of Scripture or the word of clerics.

- [There is] no clear distinction between Father, Son, and Holy Spirit. [129]

Little surprise, then, to find that his namesake educational institution emphasizes "experience," downplays the importance of scriptural details, and finds little concern with a theology stressing the "oneness" of all beings and all beliefs.

Among the names under "Past Seminars" on the University's website, we find Dan Kimball, Dallas Willard, Brian McLaren, Leonard Sweet, and Tony Campolo. [130] Lest the significance of this list be missed, note that each of these individuals is conspicuous for his connection with the emerging church movement. An illustration of this may be useful. Within the general (as opposed to religious) population of the United States, the most well known of these individuals is probably Tony Campolo, President Bill Clinton's "spiritual adviser" during the Monica Lewinsky scandal. Two short quotations from him should suffice to point out the concern:

---

129 en.wikipedia.org/wiki/George_Fox

130 georgefox.edu/seminary/news-events/ministry-contemporary-culture.html

A theology of mysticism provides some hope for common ground between Christianity and Islam. Both religions have within their histories examples of ecstatic union with God. [131]

I learned about this way of having a born-again experience from reading the Catholic mystics, especially *The Spiritual Exercises* of Ignatius of Loyola. … Like most Catholic mystics, he developed an intense desire to experience a "oneness" with God. [132]

One other name from the university's website should be mentioned: Richard Foster, the author of *Celebration of Discipline*, [133] is also listed (second only to President Herbert Hoover) under the heading, "Notable Alumni." [134]

The degree program chosen by four of the One Project's board culminates in the granting of a D.Min., a "Doctor of Ministry: Leadership and Emerging Culture." (It should be noted that the program title has more recently been changed to "Semiotics and Future Studies"). [135]

Readers may wonder if the "Emerging Culture" of this degree is somehow related to the emerging church movement. The simple answer is, yes, that is what this degree title refers to. This explains why the program was recommended by Brian McLaren. [136]

George Fox University describes Leonard Sweet as the program's "lead mentor." Other professors work with the students on a regular

---

131 Tony Campolo, *Speaking My Mind*, 149–150

132 Tony Campolo, *Letters to a Young Evangelical*, 30

133 Previously mentioned on page 75

134 georgefox.edu/about/quick_facts/index.html

135 Merriam Webster defines semiotics as "a general philosophical theory of signs and symbols that deals especially with their function in both artificially constructed and natural languages and comprises syntactics, semantics, and pragmatics." The George Fox University website says "The Doctor of Ministry in Semiotics and Future Studies program (SFS DMin) develops Christian leaders skilled at 1) anticipating the activity of Jesus in contemporary culture and 2) proactively guiding their ministries into the future." georgefox.edu/catalog/graduate/sem/programs/dmin_sfs.html

136 brianmclaren.net/archives/blog/thinking-about-a-dmin.html; more information on McLaren is found in the footnote on page 95.

basis as well, of course, but the university certainly gives Dr. Sweet top billing. [137]

This puts considerable focus on Dr. Sweet, and raises questions simply because it's not always easy to understand exactly where he may stand on certain issues. To the many Christians (both Adventist and non-Adventist) who have concerns with Dr. Sweet's teachings, the most headline-grabbing aspect of his career has clearly been his book, *Quantum Spirituality*. Published in 1991, it contains worrisome passages like this one at the close of the first chapter:

> If the church is to dance, however, it must first get its flabby self back into shape. A good place to begin is the stretching exercise of touching its TOEs. [138] Not the lungs, not the hands, not the eyes, not even the heart, but the toes may be the most important organ of the body of Christ today. So far the church has refused to dip its toe into postmodern culture. A quantum spirituality challenges the church to bear its past and to dare its future by sticking its big TOE into the time and place of the present.
>
> Then, and only then, will a flattened out, "one-dimensional," and at times dimensionless world have discovered the power and vitality of a four-dimensional faith. Then, and only then, will believers have discovered that "impossible" is a human, not a divine, category. Then, and only then, will the church not appear to be in a time capsule, sealed against new developments. Then, and only then, will a New Light movement of "world-making" faith have helped to create the world that is to, and may yet, be. Then, and only then, will earthlings have uncovered the meaning of these words, some of the last words

---

137 See, for example, georgefox.edu/seminary/programs/dmin/index.html, where the D.Min. Program is titled "Semiotics and Future Studies with Dr. Leonard Sweet."

138 In this extended metaphor which is developed throughout the first chapter, "TOE" is an acronym for "Theory of Everything." This idea, in the field of physics, is the belief that the four fundamental forces of the physical universe (magnetism, gravity, and the weak and strong atomic forces) are all the same thing. Dr. Sweet uses this imagery to imply that something similar will be found in the realm of spirituality— that all religions and belief systems will finally be found to be simply different ways of looking at the same universal truth.

poet/activist/contemplative/bridge between East and West Thomas Merton [139] uttered:

"We are already one. But we imagine that we are not. And what we have to recover is our original unity."[140]

Another example from further on in the book:

Mysticism, once cast to the sidelines of the Christian tradition, is now situated in postmodernist culture near the center. ... In the words of one of the greatest theologians of the twentieth century, Jesuit philosopher of religion/dogmatist Karl Rahner, "The Christian of tomorrow will be a mystic, one who has experienced something, or he will be nothing."[141]

One of the more striking passages in the book is a lengthy section advocating "breathing exercises." Included along the way are references to visualization (a technique common in occult activities); the literal participation of God "pouring out puffs of life into you"; the "connectedness of... not simply the human order but all creatures that breathe, including persons, plants, and animals"; and the assurance that "you have within you... the powers of goodness resident in the great spiritual leaders like Moses, Jesus, Muhammad, [and] Lao Tzu," as well as "the forces of evil and destruction."

The final "breathing exercise" seems rather reminiscent of a mass hypnotic trance, the kind of thing one might expect to see in animistic religions, but foreign to the religion of the Bible:

Gather a group together for a Navajo breathing ceremony. Stand in a circle, everyone facing the center of the circle. If there are any present in special need of prayer, ask them to "center" the circle. Place your hands in the center of the backs of those standing on either side of you and observe silence. Get in touch with one another's breathing patterns. Now breathe together as a circle, bending the knees slightly as you inhale,

---

139 See page 74

140 Leonard Sweet, *Quantum Spirituality*, 10

141 Leonard Sweet, *Quantum Spirituality*, 76

straightening up as you exhale. Keep doing this until the circle becomes one breath. [142]

In fairness, it should be pointed out that *Quantum Spirituality* was written quite a while ago. It is unfair to judge a man by words he no longer believes, and so we need to take Dr. Sweet seriously when he responded to critics of the book and said, "Would I write the same book today? No. Would I say some things differently? Yes." [143]

But it is also fair to note that Dr. Sweet never said *what* he would "say… differently." There are no recantations, retractions, or apologies. His response to his critics was written in 2010, and *Quantum Spirituality* is still for sale on the author's website. Its description reads, in part:

> Already called "a spirituality classic," *Quantum Spirituality: A Postmodern Apologetic* is the book that launched what today is called "postmodern publishing" as well as Len's ministry to postmodern culture. A book written in a circle, the reader is invited to begin anywhere, stop anytime, and end wherever. [144]

When a change in Dr. Sweet's thinking might have occurred is not specified in his Response. He did say:

> It is doubly ironic that I am under attack for being Emergent or a leader in the "emerging church" movement when I am known in emerging church circles as one of its severest critics. [145]

If that's truly the case, any change in this direction must have come after the 2002 publication of the book he co-authored with Brian D. McLaren and Jerry Haselmayer: *"A" is for Abductive: The Language of the Emerging Church.*

---

142 Leonard Sweet, *Quantum Spirituality*, 299–300

143 *A Response to Recent Misunderstandings*, leonardsweet.com/download_sad1. php?file=63_Response to Critics.pdf

144 leonardsweet.com/books.php

145 *A Response to Recent Misunderstandings*, leonardsweet.com/download_sad1. php?file=63_Response to Critics.pdf

But subsequent books do little to shore up this claim to have abandoned emergent and mystical positions. For instance, *Nudge: Awakening Each Other to the God Who's Already There*, was released in September 2010. This book—in which Sweet uses the word "nudge" as something of a synonym for "evangelism"—has this to say:

> Nudge is the Jesus in us poking the Jesus in them, but using the beings of two beloved children: us and them. …
>
> Nudge is not bringing God to people or taking Jesus to the unsaved. …
>
> Nudge is not bringing people to Jesus or introducing someone they don't know but should. Nudge is introducing people to the "Jesus in them," to the God they already know but don't know it. [146]

What does he mean, "the Jesus in them"? This can't be "Christ in you, the hope of glory,"[147] because the context is "the unsaved."

Note the following passage from one of his more recent books, *I am a Follower*, published in 2012.

> According to the book of Genesis, when God breathed spirit into matter, "man became a living being." Even today, to be fully alive is to breathe the breath of God.
>
> True followers of the way of Jesus are always aware of their breathing. They are not only in touch with the external ways of the world but also in tune with the internal sounds of life breathing around them and inside of them. They are tuning forks for others to follow their respiration.
>
> All of creation is made alive with the holy breath of the Creator. Breathing Yahweh breath is breathing the holy breath of life. Yahweh… our breathing and heartbeat are in tune with the name. Breathe in "Yah" and breathe out "weh" … I guarantee you will relax. [148]

---

146 Leonard Sweet, *Nudge: Awakening Each Other to the God Who's Already There*, 70–72

147 Colossians 1:27

148 Leonard Sweet, *I am a Follower*, 233

Apparently a mystical fascination with breath (rather like that of Ellet Waggoner's) was not a position which he abandoned since writing *Quantum Spirituality.*

Another passage from *I am a Follower:*

A life in the Spirit is a *Lectio Divina* life. These words refer to a traditional Catholic practice usually translated as "holy reading." It is often defined as "praying the Scriptures," but the discipline is actually more tied to careful listening for the voice of God. When we listen and look for the animations, ruminations, and illuminations of the Spirit, we engage in a prayer that tells God we are ready to receive the divine revelation.

Lectio divina is one example of a spiritual discipline that allows us to tune in to the reverberations and waves of the Spirit of Christ, the Spirit of love and life.[149]

With this as an introduction, Dr. Sweet provides directions for *lectio divina* from four different authorities—"the Irish-Belgian monk Dom Columba Marmion (1858–1925)," "Trappist monk Basil Pennington," "the mountain preacher," and "twelfth-century Carthusian monk Guigo II." Since it doesn't sound like a complicated process to begin with, four sets of directions should be just about sufficient for any unguarded souls who are interested in trying the "discipline" for themselves.

Perhaps it is not necessary for us to delve further into the minutia of Dr. Sweet's teachings.[150] It may be enough to simply note that he moves easily in emergent church and contemplative circles, working comfortably with Rick Warren,[151] and choosing to co-author a

---

149 Leonard Sweet, *I am a Follower,* 236

150 Others have done this at length. For fairly representative samples of the concerns expressed by others, see the following websites. Bear in mind that their perspective is not always compatible with Biblical doctrines such as the state of the dead, but there are areas in which we can agree. lighthousetrailsresearch.com, spiritual-research-network.com, or deceptioninthechurch.com.

151 Rick Warren, pastor of the Saddleback Church in Lake Forest, California, is perhaps more widely known than any of the others mentioned in this book as being in sympathy with emerging church concepts. His book, *The Purpose-Driven Life,* ("the bestselling nonfiction hardback book in history," according to Publishers Weekly) is even more widely recognized than he is. Consider that pastor Warren recommends

book with Brian McLaren (whose tendencies toward contemplative prayer and universalism make him more comfortable with an "inter-faith" identity incorporating Eastern concepts than classing himself as a Christian [152]).

Questions of Dr. Sweet's interests and activities were of little interest to Adventists as long as they were played out beyond the borders of our denomination. This seems to be changing, though, and since his influence carries with it the impression of a mysticism foreign to the Scriptures, it is fair and fitting that church members should look for clarification.

---

the book *The Soul at Rest: A Journey Into Contemplative Prayer.* With this in mind, it is hardly surprising to find that the three physicians working with Warren's Daniel Plan all embrace Eastern meditation.

152　One of McLaren's best known works is *A Generous Orthodoxy.* The front cover helps explain the general tone of the book: "Why I am a missional, evangelical, post/ protestant, liberal/conservative, mystical/poetic, Biblical, charismatic/contemplative, fundamentalist/Calvinist, Anabaptist/Anglican, Methodist, catholic, green, incarnational, depressed-yet-hopeful, emergent, unfinished Christian."

And from the back cover, we have this: "A confession and manifesto from a senior leader in the emerging church movement. *A Generous Orthodoxy* calls for a radical, Christ-centered orthodoxy of faith and practice in a missional, generous spirit. Brian McLaren argues for a post-liberal, post-conservative, post-protestant convergence."

In other words, ecumenism. And maybe a bit beyond, even. Here are two more excerpts:

"Sit down here next to me in this little restaurant and ask me if Christianity (my version of it, yours, the Pope's, whoever's) is orthodox, meaning true, and here's my honest answer: a little, but not yet. Assuming by Christianity you mean the Christian understanding of the world and God, Christian opinions on soul, text, and culture... I'd have to say that we probably have a couple of things right, but a lot of things wrong." (*A Generous Orthodoxy*, Grand Rapids: Zondervan, 2004, 164)

"Then I must add, though, that I don't believe making disciples must equal making adherents to the Christian religion. It may be advisable in many (not all!) circumstances to help people become followers of Jesus and remain within their Buddhist, Hindu, or Jewish contexts." (*A Generous Orthodoxy*, Grand Rapids: Zondervan, 2004, 260)

Chapter Twelve
Reviewing the Reviewers

ONE of the better things about shopping on the Internet is being able to read product reviews. They may not always be as rigorous as *Consumer Reports*, but there's something comforting about hearing that ordinary people like the product you're thinking to buy. Comforting, that is, until you find out that some of those online reviews are written by people with an interest in selling the product. So you learn to review the reviewers, to check out what they say to see if it rings true.

If there's one thing that deserves due diligence, it's our understanding of the Lord's will, and His plan for His church. And so, heeding the advice of Jesus Himself, we turn now—not to the verbal endorsements in behalf of emergent teachings—but to the fruits that have come from those who employ them.

It is well, just now, to pause and remember our history, to think of the care with which Ellen White sought to wield her influence so it would bless all with whom she had to deal, and perhaps especially those who were following dangerous paths. As members of God's church, we are not all individually called to deal with every issue which might afflict His cause. We are not all an Elijah, or an Isaiah, or a John the Baptist, called to deliver public rebuke for every wrong we might think we see. But we *are* called to choose our own course wisely; we *are* called to exert an influence for the truth; and we *are* called to seek to draw back any who may have wandered from the path.

We live in a tactless age, an age where anything that is "news" can spread around the world in moments, an age where the simple realities of life often deprive us of any "reasonable expectation of privacy." Still, even when issues of right and wrong are played out on a public stage— *especially* when they are played out on a public stage—there is need for graciousness in dealing with our brothers and sisters in Christ. If there is to be contention, let us contend to be most like our Savior.

The "product reviews" we are looking at, of course, are not about blenders, or all-season radials, or camera gear. We're talking about things of vastly more importance. The methods and values of the emergent church, of spiritual formation, and of contemplative prayer are new to the great majority of the Adventist church. Both those who promote them, and those who oppose them, recognize that they have not been a major part—if indeed any part at all—of our evangelistic outreach in the past. The question is simple: should we adopt these methods now?

We have looked briefly at those *outside* Adventism who advocate these principles and methods, but that investigation is important primarily because these spokesmen and their methods have been advocated by others who are *inside* Adventism. The message of the non-Adventists has, if you will, received positive reviews from members and administrators of the church. This is what now deserves our attention.

Much of the last chapter was focused on Leonard Sweet, but only because he seems to have won favor in the eyes of some Adventists. Several board members of the One Project were mentioned as ones who see value in Sweet's teachings, but the question of the emerging church and its related concepts is older and broader than this.

As Dr. Sweet has often said, we now live in a Google age, where information is merely a click away. Thus it is a fairly easy task to learn the basic history of these teachings and their introduction into Adventism. Of course, the story told is often incomplete, and there is the likelihood of considerable bias from some chroniclers, but anyone who has read online product reviews is used to this.

If we make a few arbitrary decisions restricting ourselves to the use of reputable sources, and simply searching for the main emerging church ideas and spokesmen, here are the "dots" that pop out as most notable. How we connect these dots is, of course, a matter of individual judgment.

A simple search of the General Conference Office of Archives website, looking for the names of prominent advocates of emerging church theology yields one surprisingly early outlier—an article from 1985 which approvingly cites Richard Foster (three times), Saint John of the Cross, Thomas Merton, and Henri Nouwen (twice)—as well as Martin Luther, Charles Spurgeon, and Ellen White! [153] As

---

153 Rick Trott, "New Dimensions in Prayer," *Atlantic Union Gleaner*, April 23, 1985; docs. adventistarchives.org/docs/ALUG/ALUG19850423-V84-08__C.pdf#view=fit

seems to be common for Adventists with an interest in these authors, the writer of this article was a chaplain in an Adventist college. He served in this capacity for twenty years before accepting a position as a professor of religion and chaplaincy, eventually rising to chair of the Religion and Theology Department of the college.[154] Simple searches of the Internet provided no information as to whether or not he remained positive on the work of Foster, Merton, and Nouwen.

Skipping over a number of apparently inconsequential references to the basic ideas or prominent authors of the mystical movement, we pass on to the formation of a new organization. The Leadership Institute (a "doing business as" entity of College & Career Ministries Inc, located in Orange, California), is one of the most intriguing examples of Adventist interest in the broad range of emerging church ideas.

Founded in 1989,[155] The Leadership Institute (TLI) is directed by L. Paul Jensen. The organization's website says that Jensen is "an Adjunct Assistant Professor of Leadership and Christian Formation and Spirituality in Contemporary Culture at Fuller Theological Seminary. He has served on the staff of Campus Crusade for Christ and pioneered campus ministries and trained campus chaplains for the Adventist Church. Paul was a graduate visiting student under N.T. Wright at Oxford University."[156]

The website does not completely answer the traditional journalistic questions of when, where, who, how, and why Dr. Jensen worked with these Adventist campus chaplains. We are simply told that "he and his wife, Cheris, served on the staff of Campus Crusade for Christ (now CRU) and pioneered campus ministries in the Adventist Church for a total of sixteen years before starting the Institute in 1989." If we make the (unconfirmed) assumption that these sixteen years were consecutive and immediately prior to the founding of TLI, that would take us back to 1973.[157]

---

154 *Atlantic Union Gleaner*, April 2011, 12; atlantic-union.org/wordpress/wp-content/uploads/2012/08/Apr11Gleaner.pdf

155 spiritualleadership.com

156 spiritualleadership.com/about-us/our-staff-team

157 Additional information could, no doubt, be tracked down. Something as simple as a telephone call to the Leadership Institute might well supply more facts, but our purpose is not to play private detective so much as to examine the "postmodern" thumbnail sketch produced by simple key-punching and mouse-clicking on Google. Of course, like every

One thing the website does make clear on its "Our Team" page is that the organization has close connections to Fuller Theological Seminary. Of the eleven team members, six graduated with advanced degrees from Fuller, and four have served as faculty members there. [158]

The other five team members have degrees or credentials from Pepperdine University, Denver Theological Seminary, the Graduate Theological Foundation, Azusa Pacific University, the Talbot School of Theology, and the Monastery of the Risen Christ.

Of particular note is Jon Ciccarelli (the Azusa Pacific graduate), who is described as "senior pastor at the Calimesa Seventh-day Adventist Church." [159]

One might wonder about the relationship of the Leadership Institute to the organized Seventh-day Adventist Church, were it not for helpful coverage of that aspect by *Adventist Today*. In an informative article by Dr. Merle Whitney, [160] we are told:

---

other business in the world today, LTI does have a Facebook page, though it seems to be something of a "lite" version of the website.

158 For comparison, only eight of the fifty-one "Regular Faculty" of the Seventh-day Adventist Theological Seminary at Andrews University have advanced degrees from Fuller. andrews.edu/academics/bulletin/2012-2013/18personnel/18-09-sem-faculty.pdf

This circumstance brings to mind a quotation from a prominent Seventh-day Adventist leader from some decades back. Elder L.E. Froom, founding editor of *Ministry* magazine, once asked:

"How dare a man contemplate, or have the temerity to present, the degree of doctor of divinity, gained in the universities of Babylon, as a credential for teaching or preaching this threefold message, the second stipulation of which is, "Babylon is fallen, is fallen. … Come out of her my people"?

"How dare we accept such a Babylonian credential in lieu of mastery of the truth? Shall a man go into Babylon to gain strength and wisdom to call men out of Babylon? To ask the question is but to disclose how far some have compromised with Babylon, as they have gone back to Babylon to drink from her wells of wisdom. Oh, for the living waters of truth fresh from the Word!

"Someone needs to sound an alarm. We need to grip ourselves and halt a growing trend that, if it becomes entrenched, will bring disaster through neutralizing our message." *The Ministry*, April 1944, 13, 30

159 spiritualleadership.com/about-us/our-staff-team

160 Dr. Whitney is identified by the biographical information at the end of the article as the "pastor of the Anaheim Seventh-day Adventist Church, Anaheim, California."

The Task Force to Reach the Next Generation was set up by the administrators of the Southeastern California Conference in response to strong direction from the Conference Executive Committee to reach and retain youth and young adults. Very significant funding was provided in the conference budget beginning in 1993 and has continued each year since. Almost immediately the task force became known as the Boomer/Buster Project. As additional groups of pastors were formed, the "official" name became The Journey to Reach the Next Generations (note added plural), and most participants and leaders now refer to the process simply as "The Journey."

Paul Jensen, director of the Leadership Institute, and an ordained Adventist minister, was commissioned to direct and facilitate the task force. ...

As of this writing [2002] ten groups have been formed that have included both Adventist and other pastors. ...

Three times each year participants in The Journey meet for a three-day retreat at Pine Springs Ranch, the Southeastern California Conference camp and conference center in the San Jacinto mountains. ...

Soon after the process began, its "subversive" nature became apparent. ... On one retreat we would study and discuss, go back to our churches to practice what we had learned in specific projects, and on the next retreat report on progress made (or the lack of it) and evaluate with each other what was occurring and why. However, the foundation for The Journey was the spiritual formation of the pastors involved in the process. Soon this became an important aspect of recruiting subsequent groups.[161]

Whitney's *Adventist Today* article was written in 2002, nine years after the founding of TLI. Is the Southeastern California Conference

---

161 *Adventist Today*, Nov.–Dec. 2002, 22; atoday.org/issue_pdf.php?pdf=2002-06.pdf. Two other articles about TLI and The Journey (written by Ken Curtis, then the associate pastor of the Calimesa Seventh-day Adventist Church, and Greg and Linda Clark) appear in the same issue.

still supporting the Leadership Institute? There is little information to clarify the working relationship between the Institute and the Conference. A search of the SECC website for "Paul Jensen" yields no hits.[162] The only item of any note was this one sentence, written from the perspective of Pine Springs Ranch:

> We are privileged to host the Leadership Institute as they nurture the souls of many of SECC's pastors through the ministry of The Journey (a program of spiritual formation and renewal for conference leaders).[163]

Since this is something which appears to be an influence on "the souls of many of SECC's pastors," their parishioners might conceivably wish to know more about the Leadership Institute in general, and what all is involved in The Journey in particular. It seems curious that so little is said.

The Leadership Institute is a not-for-profit organization recognized by the Internal Revenue Service. With this privilege comes certain legal responsibilities and a degree of scrutiny by a variety of "charity watch dog" organizations. A number of these organizations provide another interesting perspective on the relationship of TLI to the SECC.

According to the organization's annual non-profit filings for the years 2006 through 2013, one member of TLI's board of directors is an individual listed as "Sandy Roberts."[164]

The name "Sandy" is slightly ambiguous. Wikipedia says:

> Sandy is a popular unisex name; the male version can be a diminutive of "Alexander," "Alasdair," "Sandipan," "Sanford," or "Santiago," while the female version is a diminutive for "Sandra" or less commonly "Alexandra" and "Cassandra."[165]

---

162 A search of the current Seventh-day Adventist Yearbook yields no hits for a Paul Jensen, either, so it would appear that he is not currently employed by the church. See adventistyearbook.org/default. aspx?page=SearchResults&Search=jensen&Year=9999&AdmFieldID=NAD

163 secc.adventistfaith.org/news_entries/6363

164 nccsdataweb.urban.org/orgs/profile/330019749?popup=1#forms

165 en.wikipedia.org/wiki/Sandy_(given_name)

But the address given with the name—11330 Pierce Street, Riverside, CA 92505—helps narrow this down. That's the address for the Southeastern California Conference, the work address, rather than the home address, of Sandra Roberts. At the time she joined the board of directors for the Leadership Institute, she was employed as the Executive Secretary of the Southeastern California Conference. After nine years in that position, however, her title changed on October 27, 2013:

> To loud applause Sunday afternoon, Dr. Sandra Roberts was confirmed as Southeastern California Conference's next president, making her the first Adventist woman to be elected as a conference president. The history-making vote (567 "yes" to 219 "no" or 72% to 28%) overwhelmingly affirmed the conference nominating committee's recommendation despite a cautionary message from General Conference president Ted N.C. Wilson.[166]

In one sense, it is not surprising that Sandra Roberts should serve as a link between TLI and the Conference. According to the biographical information which appeared on the SECC's website during her tenure as Executive Secretary, she—

> Earned a Doctor of Ministry degree, with emphasis in spiritual formation, from the Claremont School of Theology.[167]

This education would presumably make her better able to judge the effectiveness of the training provided for the pastors of the conference.

Some additional information as to the working relationship between the two organizations shows up in another Google search:[168]

---

166 spectrummagazine.org/blog/2013/10/27/
sandra-roberts-becomes-first-woman-president

167 web.archive.org/web/20110811182151/http://seccsecretariat.adventistfaith.org/
The more recent biographical posting, used since she was elected president of the conference, describes the degree as "a Doctor of Ministry degree, with emphasis in leadership development and spirituality." We assume the slightly different wording is inconsequential, as both versions must surely describe the same academic course. Some information regarding her thesis for this program can be found here: phdtree.org/pdf/25521665-postmoderns-most-wanted-using-a-spiritual-formation-process-of-volunteer-youth-leadership-development-in-a-seventh-day-adventist-conference/

168 Search for: spiritualleadership.org "secc journey"

In November 2013, the Journey celebrated its 20th anniversary in the Southeastern Conference of Adventists (Generation 1 had their first retreat in November 1993). On the strength of twenty years of training nearly 125 pastors from the conference, we believe that there is an opportunity to significantly increase the scope and impact of the Journey over the next few years. [169]

As one would expect, the document goes on to propose a variety of plans and options as to how TLI might continue working with the pastors of the SECC. But we have yet to examine any indication as to what the training offered the SECC pastors might include. A quick look through the documents Google finds on the TLI website gives some details:[170]

- One whole category of "Courses, Retreats, Seminars, [and] Workshops" offered by The Leadership Institute in 2012 was entitled "Nouwen Legacy: Celebrating Henri Nouwen's Spiritual Impact." These opportunities included two different eight-week online classes; one twelve-session class taught for Fuller Theological Seminary; two three-day retreats; two one-day retreats; one three-day, one two-day, and one one-day workshop; a one-day seminar; and a half-day lecture. The schedule for 2013 did not include the two eight-week courses, but had a greater number of shorter events. All these various presentations focused on the perceived value of Henri Nouwen's work.

- A number of documents available on the website seem designed to introduce spiritual formation to those unfamiliar with it, especially Protestants. One example reads: "One gift to the church that has been little known among Protestants until recently is the prayer of Examen. This prayer was introduced to members of the Society of Jesus (Jesuits) by its founder Ignatius of Loyola (1491–1556). It was a primary form of prayer for the Society, which was founded as a missionary order. As a spiritual practice that can be done anytime anywhere, it is especially accessible to mobile

---

169 *A Proposed Future for the SECC Journey*; spiritualleadership.com/wp-content/uploads/SECC-Journey-Proposal.pdf

170 spiritualleadership.com/resources/
spiritualleadership.com/wp-content/uploads/JourneyIntroBrochureOnline.pdf

and busy people in the workplace, even as it was for the early Jesuits who went throughout the world as itinerant missionaries to establish evangelistic work and colleges." [171]

- Throughout the website and its various documents, we find a number of phrases which raise concern. Among these are such terms as "desert spirituality" (a reference to the "desert fathers") and "contemplative evangelism." This latter is especially worrisome in light of the many testimonies of those who have been affected by the overpowering emotional impact of coming into direct contact with an unarguably supernatural power through "contemplative," "meditative," or "visualization" practices.

- There are frequent references to *lectio divina* (and a variation focusing on images rather than sounds, for which they have coined the phrase *visio divina*).

- One document tells of an individual's experience while walking the path of a labyrinth, and how "God" spoke a series of two-word phrases to her: "I AM... you are... We are... they are... everything is... I AM." [172]

- References to other sources to which one may turn for further information are common. As a general matter, these are troubling, for they prominently feature all the main expositors of the fully developed contemplative practices of the emerging church movement. Among the contemporary authors most frequently cited are Henri Nouwen, Thomas Merton, Dallas Willard, Eugene Peterson, and Paul Jensen's former professor, N.T. Wright. Among the "classical" authors are found Ignatius Loyola, St. John of the Cross, Teresa of Avila, and Thomas à Kempis. One particularly troubling name given as a resource is that of Sue Monk Kidd. [173]

Sue Monk Kidd is a writer of some note, but our interest is in her spiritual transition. She began as a conservative Baptist... and then

---

171 spiritualleadership.com/Prayer-of-Examen/

172 spiritualleadership.com/wp-content/uploads/2013/02/EPC_Journal_samples.pdf, 3

173 spiritualleadership.com/wp-content/uploads/TLI-Spiritual-Direction.pdf

a friend gave her a book by Thomas Merton. Here is her story in her own words:

> Merton's writings were perhaps the most formative works I've ever read. His famous autobiographical book, *The Seven Storey Mountain*, written when he was a young man, had a life-altering effect on me when I read it at the age of twenty-nine. ... The book revealed to me the startling reality of the inner life, cracking open a raw longing for the Divine and exposing an irrepressible hunger for that deepest thing in myself. [174]

This introduction to contemplative life had a profound effect on her. Her perceptions, beliefs, and expectations all changed drastically. It's really no surprise that she finally "found" what she was looking for:

> Today I remember that event for the radiant mystery it was, how I felt myself embraced by Goddess, how I felt myself in touch with the deepest thing I am. It was the moment when, as playwright and poet Ntozake Shange put it, "I found god in myself/ and I loved her/ I loved her fiercely." [175]

Today she advocates a sort of Unitarian, panentheistic Goddess worship:

> Goddess forces us... to take our human lives in our arms and clasp it for the divine life it is. ...

> We will discover the Divine deep within the earth and the cells of our bodies, and we will love her there with all our hearts and all our souls and all our minds. [176]

But how did this happen? Perhaps her most revealing comment in this regard is the following vignette, set in the middle of a church service:

---

174 suemonkkidd.com/Firstlight/Excerpts.aspx

175 Sue Monk Kidd, *The Dance of the Dissident Daughter*, 136

176 Sue Monk Kidd, *The Dance of the Dissident Daughter*, 161

The minister was preaching. He was holding up a Bible. It was open, perched atop his raised hand as if a blackbird had landed there. He was saying that the Bible was the sole and ultimate authority of the Christian's life. The *sole* and *ultimate* authority.

I remember a feeling rising up from a place about two inches below my navel. It was a passionate, determined feeling, and it spread out from the core of me like a current so that my skin vibrated with it. If feelings could be translated into English, this feeling would have roughly been the word *no!*

It was the purest inner knowing I had experienced, and it was shouting in me *no, no, no!* The ultimate authority of my life is not the Bible; it is not confined between the covers of a book. It is not something written by men and frozen in time. It is not from a source outside myself. *My ultimate authority is the divine voice in my own soul.* Period. [177]

Now the original point of mentioning Sue Monk Kidd was to express concern that the Leadership Institute lists her as an appropriate source for understanding the material presented in The Journey. Did they make a terribly unfortunate mistake in listing a source not in harmony with their teaching, or is their teaching a terribly unfortunate mistake?

There are yet two other points worth drawing out of her account. The seemingly invariable result of mystical, contemplative activity is the sense that the human is divine, and that everyone and everything is "One." From the accounts of the mystics, it seems this sense of oneness is the most enthralling aspect of the experience.[178] Here is another example from Monk Kidd:

Have you ever tried looking at another person and seeing your own self within him or her? I don't mean projecting onto another person all our miserable traits. I am speaking of recognizing the hidden truth that we are one with all people. We are part of them and they are part of us.

---

177 Sue Monk Kidd, *The Dance of the Dissident Daughter*, 76; emphasis hers.

178 See comments by Nouwen (page 75–76), Campolo (page 8–89)8, and Merton (page 91).

Frederick Buechner spoke of growing to a point where "self-hood, in the sense that you are one self and I am another self, begins to fade. You begin to understand that in some way your deepest self is the self of all men—that you are in them and they are in you."[179]

The second point that these passages illustrate is the loss of balance between the Inspired Word of God and the Incarnate Word of God. The contemplative approach elevates the subjective, emotional, "spiritual" experience of contact with what is believed to be God, until it is out of balance and proportion with the more objective instruction of Scripture. Both a personal relationship with Christ and a submission to the authority of the written Word are essential, but neither is safe if taken to the exclusion of the other. This issue is clearly addressed in the Spirit of Prophecy:

> Through all Scripture, in both the Old and the New Testaments, Christ himself speaks; for he is the Word of God. [180]

> Those who read and listen to the sophistries that prevail in this age do not know God as He is. They contradict the Word of God, and extol and worship nature in the place of the Creator. While we may discern the working of God in the things He has created, these things are not God. [181]

> We are rapidly approaching the close of this world's history. Every moment is of the most solemn importance to the child of God. The questions that should come to every heart are, "Am I a Christian? Is the word of God my study? Is Christ dwelling in my heart by faith? Is the law of God the rule of my life? Do the searching truths I profess to believe, penetrate into the very secret places of my life?"[182]

---

179 Sue Monk Kidd, *God's Joyful Surprise*, 233

180 *Review and Herald*, February 12, 1889

181 *Manuscript Releases*, vol. 7, 372

182 *Review and Herald*, September 25, 1888

Forty-five years ago, when I commenced my labors, we met many erroneous doctrines. One and another would say, "I have the truth, because my feelings tell me so." Others declared that they were led of the Spirit; but there are two spirits in the world—the Spirit of God and the spirit of Satan. We are not left to be guided by the uncertainty of feelings, nor by the deceptive spirit of error. Here is the word of God. Christ declared, "Thy word is truth;" and the Spirit that Christ promised to his disciples, was to lead them into all truth. Then can we not test what spirit we are of? If we are led into harmony with the explicit commands of God, we have the Spirit of truth. These I have spoken of had gone beyond the need of their Bibles; they had left that for those not so far advanced as themselves. As I endeavored to reason with them, with my Bible in hand, they pushed me away, unwilling that their errors should be tried; "but he that doeth truth cometh to the light, that his deeds may be made manifest, that they are wrought in God." We want to know "what saith the Scriptures." Let God be true, but every man a liar. He has declared the conditions of eternal life, and we want to know that we are complying with them, and are preparing for the world to come. [183]

The union of the divine and the human, manifest in Christ, exists also in the Bible. The truths revealed are all "given by inspiration of God;" yet they are expressed in the words of men and are adapted to human needs. Thus it may be said of the Book of God, as it was of Christ, that "the Word was made flesh, and dwelt among us." And this fact, so far from being an argument against the Bible, should strengthen faith in it as the word of God. Those who pronounce upon the inspiration of the Scriptures, accepting some portions as divine while they reject other parts as human, overlook the fact that Christ, the divine, partook of our human nature, that He might reach humanity. In the work of God for man's redemption, divinity and humanity are combined. [184]

---

183 *Signs of the Times*, November 24, 1887

184 *Testimonies*, vol. 5, 747

One final observation on the Leadership Institute and its director comes to us from the website of Spring Arbor University. In an advertisement for their Master of Arts in Spiritual Formation and Leadership degree, the speakers from previous sessions are listed, presumably to indicate the quality of the program. We simply note that L. Paul Jensen [presenting the topic *Spirituality, Leadership, and The Collapse of Space and Time*] is listed on a par with John Michael Talbot [*On Being a Monk in the World: The Way of the New Monasticism*], Tony Campolo [*Spirituality and Social Justice*], Shane Claiborne [*Spirituality and Social Justice*], Dallas Willard [*Intensive Seminar in Spiritual Formation*], and Richard J. Foster [*Intensive Seminar in Spiritual Formation*].

One thought which deserves consideration is the possibility that all these concerns are built on nothing but a charge of guilt by association. It would be possible to make that case against the final item above. After all, Jensen is simply listed on the same web page as the other individuals; that hardly proves he agrees with them in all things.

True enough. If one should choose to do so, the final item above may be stricken from the record. But not the others. There is a difference between guilt by association and guilt from recommendation. If I were to repeatedly recommend that others try eating wild mushrooms—citing my Ph.D. in Mycology as reason to trust my judgment—and never so much as whisper that there may be something deadly about some of them, it could not be called slander to point out the danger of such a course and the culpability of such a recommendation.

Chapter Thirteen
The Extending Influence

BEFORE anything more is said on this topic, it should be explicitly stated that this book does not contend that the Leadership Institute is solely responsible for the emerging church and contemplative, mystical teachings knocking at the door of the Seventh-day Adventist Church.

Such an assertion is certainly not supportable from the simple "postmodern" Google searching reported here. This volume simply contends that there is ample evidence of such ideas being introduced into the church; that anyone with access to the Internet and a little curiosity can check for themselves; and that those teachings are foreign to Adventism. Others may investigate further if they are so inclined.

And so—with no intent to imply any direct connection to the Leadership Institute—we move on now to consider another significant proponent of emerging church concepts. Again, we simply present the findings of the world's favorite search engine.

In the November 11, 2010, issue of the *Adventist Review*, the "Tools of the Trade" column written by Monte Sahlin announced a "new discipleship resource." Impressively large in scope and size, the resource is "called *iFollow*... because it is largely an electronic system published on DVD and via a website, and its focus is 'I follow Jesus.' It's a resource designed for pastors and lay leaders in local churches to use in small groups, seminars, midweek meetings, new member classes, and one-on-one."

It is clear from the description that this was not a minor undertaking, nor a project carried out without serious—and creative— thought. One aim was to provide tools that would be more specifically designed to reach different classes of people:

It includes materials designed for "pre-Christians," unchurched people who have some interest in spiritual things but have not made a commitment to follow Jesus, new Christians who want to study Adventist beliefs, and longer-term members learning various ministry skills and developing leadership abilities.

On the general principle that it's a good thing to have different tools fitted for different jobs, this approach has much to be commended. As to the program's scope of coverage, the announcement said:

> More than 100 units are included in the original release. Each unit has a presenter's guide, handouts for participants, discussion questions for groups, learning activities, and a PowerPoint presentation. The presenter's guide for each unit also includes a list of additional resources related to the particular topic. These tools are all designed to help local leaders encourage and support church members and others in learning to give their lives more fully to Christ and grow in their discipleship.

By any measure, this is a major contribution to the toolbox of the local pastor or church member who is looking for materials to use in the work of soul-winning. And more than soul-*winning*. One might say that the program is also designed for soul-*growing*.

One innovative aspect of this program is that it is intended to not only provide Bible studies for use with non-Adventists, but also—as just noted—materials intended for use with even long-time church members.

> The complete set of materials addresses the whole of life and seeks to equip believers to share the gifts that Jesus has given them.

Roughly speaking, the purpose and goal expressed above is about the same as some definitions and explanations of spiritual formation. In what is said, there is nothing to cause concern. Any Adventist should be able to say a hearty "amen" to this goal—within the context of God's truth for these last days, there is nothing wrong here. Unfortunately, circumstances being what they are in the world and in the church, it is still wise to consider the content of the *iFollow* program to see what it offers us.

Fortunately, this is easy to do, since—as the *Adventist Review* announcement went on to say—

Anyone who is interested can. … download the original set of materials on the DVD, as well as regular releases of new materials as they are developed.[185]

The website in question here is ifollowdiscipleship.org, and the materials are, indeed, freely available. That being the case, it's a simple matter to search their contents. These are the results from searches for the major proponents of the emerging church practices:

- Henri Nouwen—fourteen citations, one book recommended once, website listed

- N.T. Wright—nine citations, four different books recommended a total of twenty-one times, website listed once

- Brian McLaren—six citations, five different books recommended a total of twenty-four times

- Leonard Sweet—four citations, one book recommendation, website listed once

- Richard Foster—three citations, two different books recommended a total of sixteen times, website listed five times

- Dallas Willard—two citations, six different books recommended a total of sixty-six times

- Bill Hybels—one citation, four different books recommended a total of eleven times

- Eugene Peterson—one citation, one book recommended once[186]

---

185 *Adventist Review*, November 11, 2010, 28; archives.adventistreview.org/issue_pdf. php?issue=2010-1536

186 The one citation from Peterson is as follows:

Isaiah 58:13–14 is particularly instructive in *The Message*, translated from the original Hebrew by many-years-experienced Hebrew scholar Eugene Peterson: "'If you watch your step on the Sabbath and don't use my holy day for personal advantage, if you treat the Sabbath as a day of joy, God's holy day as a celebration, if you honor it by refusing "business as usual," making money, running here and there—then you'll be free to enjoy God! Oh, I'll make you ride high and soar above it all. I'll make you feast on the inheritance of your ancestor Jacob.' Yes! God says so!"

Peterson's translation of Scripture is a particularly ironic resource to be listed in a Bible study, considering he said this:

- Tony Jones—never cited, but one book recommended fourteen times [187]

- And, if we move beyond personal names in our searching we find the following terms:

- Silence—twenty-two times

- Meditation—one hundred thirty-eight times

It should be stated that the raw count for the term "meditation" was somewhat inflated because the word was used in the title of a side-bar on each page of one of the studies. Since that particular study is twenty-one pages long, the number is given as one hundred thirty-eight occurrences rather than the one hundred fifty-nine actually returned by the computer search.

Again, the reason for considering these figures is because they are *recommendations*. We might overlook a few matters here and there, assuming them to not be in harmony with the recommenders' views, but here we have scores of recommendations leading to material well beyond anything directly espoused in the lessons themselves, and yet not a single word of caution.

We are left with the perplexing question as to whether the editors of the *iFollow* materials simply failed to indicate that "these materials do not in all regards reflect the views of the editors," or if they actually *do* reflect the editors' views.

This question is compounded by the editors' pointed efforts to defend some of the questionable methodologies they advocate in the

---

"Well, why do people spend so much time studying the Bible? How much do you need to know? We invest all this time in understanding the text which has a separate life of it's own and we think we're being more pious and spiritual when we're doing it. But it's all to be lived. It was given to us so we could live it. But most Christians know far more of the Bible than they're living. They should be studying it less, not more. You just need enough to pay attention to God." (*Mars Hill Review*, Fall 1995, Issue No. 3) leaderu.com/marshill/mhr03/peter1.html

187 The book recommended is *The Sacred Way: Spiritual Practices for Everyday Life*. A look at its table of contents is instructive—*Part I: Introduction*; 1. The Quest for God. 2.What is Spirituality and How Do You Practice It? *Part II: Via Contemplativa: Contemplative Approaches to Spirituality*; 3. Silence and Solitude. 4. Sacred Reading. 5. The Jesus Prayer. 6. Centering Prayer. 7. Meditation. 8. The Ignatian Examen. 9. Icons. 10. Spiritual Direction. 11. Daily Office. *Part III: Via Activa: Bodily Approaches to Spirituality*; 12. The Labyrinth. 13. Stations of the Cross. 14. Pilgrimage. 15. Fasting. 16. The Sign of the Cross and Other Bodily Prayers. 17. Sabbath. 18. Service.

lessons. In many cases, the line of reasoning presented opens the door for activities beyond anything actually spelled out in the *iFollow* lessons. This is worrisome, since it seems to be a perfect means of paving the road to the more extreme spiritual exercises advocated in the recommended books and websites.

But first things first; here are a few examples of the practices directly encouraged in the *iFollow* materials:

> One essential is meditation. This refers to the mental practice of emptying the mind, quieting the chatter of my thoughts, and entering into mindfulness. I recommend doing it for two periods a day, about 20 minutes in the morning and again in the evening. I sit in an alert manner and concentrate on slowing my breathing. Distractions are noted and let go as I focus on inner quiet. [188]

There is a curious contradiction here that crops up several times in the lessons. Meditation is first called "emptying the mind," but moments later it is described as "entering into mindfulness." This is puzzling. If the mind is "empty," wouldn't it be more correct to describe the condition as "mind*less*ness"? In another passage describing this process, we are told that "it takes practice to shift into neutral."[189]

The editors make frequent efforts to differentiate the meditation promoted in the lessons from what they call "Eastern" or "New Age" meditation. Unfortunately, the differences often seem artificial.

> Others may try to meditate on nothingness or empty their mind, but Christians must meditate on something, actually, Someone. Fix Jesus' face in your mind's eye. Don't worry, He knows you don't know what He really looks like, and He doesn't mind how you imagine Him.[190]

The mental image of an imagined face has very little actual substance. Within Catholic, Buddhist, and New Age mysticism, it is

---

188 *Mission Group Process, Part Three: Developing a Covenant*, 6; 216.122.106.61/resource.aspx?id=2872&chk=159682982

189 *Spiritual Disciplines: Meditation*, 6; 216.122.106.61/resource.aspx?id=2836&chk=159417410

190 *Spiritual Disciplines: Meditation*, 7; 216.122.106.61/resource.aspx?id=2836&chk=159417410

common to focus one's gaze on the flame of a candle. There's not much substance there, either, but at least you can actually see it. Once again, any difference from the forms of meditation that the lessons acknowledge to be dangerous is overshadowed by the similarities. It seems a stretch to believe that what is advocated here is not functionally the same as the activities that are warned against.

In the middle of a section dealing with worship forms and activities, the lessons admonish us that

> It is important to remember the Seventh-day Adventist Church does not have a set liturgy. Adventists have believed, since the beginning, in what is called "free" worship. Ellen G. White writes on many occasions that she and others were given "freedom" as they led in worship.[191]

This argument is a wholesale misrepresentation of the "many occasions" mentioned. When Ellen White says she "had freedom in speaking," or writes that she "spoke with freedom for one hour," she certainly is not addressing matters of liturgy. A much simpler interpretation finds support in the 1828 version of Noah Webster's American Dictionary included on the E.G. White Writings CD-ROM:

> "Freedom, n. … 6. Ease or facility of doing any thing. He speaks or acts with freedom. 7. Frankness; boldness. He addressed his audience with freedom."

The manner in which the lesson says that Ellen White was "given 'freedom,'" implies that the church members let her do whatever she wanted in terms of liturgy. A simple search of the CD-ROM[192] yields two hundred twenty-five examples of such a comment, not one of which has anything to do with liturgy. Thirty-eight of these examples explicitly state that it was the Lord who gave this freedom.

It is worth noting that this misrepresentation is a strained effort to support an amoral view of music and dance. The lessons take pains to *oppose* the view that "there are kinds of music which

---

191 *Member Care: Reconnecting*, 7; 216.122.106.61/resource.
aspx?id=2869&chk=159660851

192 Enter this text for the search, including quotation marks: "freedom spoke"@8 or "freedom speaking"@4

are intrinsically right or wrong." This position is taken in regard to worship styles, the editors asserting that, "in fact the Bible nowhere condemns any of these methods of praise. Instead, it condemns false principles and theology." [193]

This is painting with an extremely wide brush! One might also say that the praise of human sacrifice is acceptable, too, as long as it's not carried out with false principles or theology! The reality is that methodology can never be entirely disconnected from principles and theology, and it must be evaluated in that light.

This issue, and other points to come in later chapters, call for honest consideration of Ellen White's comments concerning the "liturgy" of the meetings held in Indiana during the fanatical Holy Flesh Movement of 1900. It is very difficult to believe her concerns were limited to abstract principles and theology!

> The things you have described as taking place in Indiana, the Lord has shown me would take place just before the close of probation. Every uncouth thing will be demonstrated. There will be shouting, with drums, music, and dancing. The senses of rational beings will become so confused that they cannot be trusted to make right decisions. And this is called the moving of the Holy Spirit.

> The Holy Spirit never reveals itself in such methods, in such a bedlam of noise. This is an invention of Satan to cover up his ingenious methods for making of none effect the pure, sincere, elevating, ennobling, sanctifying truth for this time. Better never have the worship of God blended with music than to use musical instruments to do the work which last January was represented to me would be brought into our camp meetings. The truth for this time needs nothing of this kind in its work of converting souls. A bedlam of noise shocks the senses and perverts that which if conducted aright might be a blessing. The powers of satanic agencies blend with the din and noise, to have a carnival, and this is termed the Holy Spirit's working. ...

---

193 *Spiritual Disciplines: Worship*, 6; 216.122.106.61/resource.
aspx?id=2848&chk=159505934

No encouragement should be given to this kind of worship. The same kind of influence came in after the passing of the time in 1844. The same kind of representations were made. Men became excited, and were worked by a power thought to be the power of God. [194]

Note the reference to the fanaticism which followed the passing of the 2300 Days in 1844. It would seem that the account of the meeting she had read brought to mind the same memories as did her reading of *The Living Temple*. It's impossible to see that as a positive endorsement.

This next series of excerpts is from the directions provided for the facilitator of a group activity designed to "drive home the concept that prayer is a two-way conversation":

Say the group will get a chance to practice two-way prayer with a Biblical meditation. They will imagine they are personally present at the scene of [whatever miracle you have chosen] and will be able to talk to Jesus about it and see what insights or blessings are revealed to them.

The question here is the *source* of whatever is "revealed to" the participants. Those "insights or blessings" must come from somewhere. The implication of being "able to talk to Jesus" is clearly that He will reply, hence "Christ" would be the source. This activity is, after all, supposed to "drive home the concept that prayer is a two-way conversation."

The instructions continue:

Read the following sentence by Ellen White from *Thoughts from the Mount of Blessing*: "Let us in imagination go back to that scene, and … enter into the thoughts and feelings that filled their hearts. Understanding what the words of Jesus meant to those who heard them, we may discern in them a new vividness and beauty, and may also gather for ourselves their deeper lessons."

---

194 *Selected Messages*, Book Two, 37

The method suggested in this quotation is, of course, entirely different from that in the exercise. Ellen White encourages her readers to consider the point of view of the original hearers as a means of more clearly understanding Christ's instruction. Her intent is *not* to "talk to Jesus" and receive *new* instruction.

The exercise continues:

> Have them get comfortable and close their eyes. Tell them to try to imagine they are in Palestine in the time of Jesus. If the story you have in mind is in a particular season or place, let them know that. If they wish to try to imagine what it might have been like to be some particular person at the scene, they may do so, or they may simply be themselves, observing the miracle. Allowing them time to think about it, ask them to imagine what they might see (wait) hear (wait), touch (wait), smell (wait), and (if applicable) taste. Give a minute between each, for them to set the scene in their minds. Then, tell the story simply. Ask them to have a two-way conversation with Jesus about what they've just experienced, and remain silent for at least five minutes. [195]

This is classic guided imagery, a well-established technique for quieting the thoughts and opening the mind to receive input from an external spirit source. The *iFollow* materials contest this point, asserting that

> This is different from what is commonly called "guided imagery," in which a leader actually guides what the participants are to imagine, think, or "see." What would be the dangers, if any, and how does Biblical meditation guard against those dangers? [196]

The concern expressed in regard to guided imagery given here is simply inaccurate; the danger is not from the content of what a leader might tell the participants to imagine, it's from the relaxed mental state which opens the way for the possible mental/emotional/spiritual impact of a supernatural response from an undeniably external

---

195 *Recovery Ministry, Step Eleven: Keep in Touch*, 10; 216.122.106.61/resource. aspx?id=2898&chk=159874784

196 *Spiritual Disciplines: Meditation*, 16; 216.122.106.61/resource. aspx?id=2836&chk=159417410

source. This doesn't always happen with guided imagery, of course, just as Ouija boards don't always exhibit supernatural behavior—but that's no reason to play with either.

Consider two more passages:

> Once a converted, saved, growing, forgiven child of God learns how to see the Bible in a personal light and read all the precious old stories as if they really were written for him, then he is ready to discover the next step. He is ready to learn how he can talk to God and "hear" God's answer just like all those people in the Bible did. [197]

> Sitting quietly in meditation helps us learn to really listen. We may not hear a voice when God speaks to us, but quieting the chatter will let us hear God. [198]

It is difficult to say just what expectations the editors hoped to raise with these comments. It would have been appropriate to insert some acknowledgment that the prophets of old who heard God's voice didn't do so on their own schedule through means of their own arranging, but there is nothing of the sort.

An expectation that "I am going to hear God" is not a healthy frame of mind. At best, it will lead to disappointment; at worst, it will lead to satanic deception. We've seen this quotation before, but it bears repeating as a caution in this context:

> We need not the mysticism that is in this book [*Living Temple*]. Those who entertain these sophistries will soon find themselves in a position where the enemy can talk with them, and lead them away from God. [199]

Though there are serious concerns to address here, we can certainly be thankful for these two comments from the *iFollow* editors:

---

197 *Spiritual Disciplines: Meditation*, 8; 216.122.106.61/resource. aspx?id=2836&chk=159417410

198 *Spiritual Disciplines: Meditation*, 2; 216.122.106.61/resource. aspx?id=2836&chk=159417410

199 *Review and Herald*, October 22, 1903

God is never going to give you guidance that disagrees with His already-recorded Word.[200]

God will not set aside His revealed Word, least of all His own law, to suit you![201]

Perhaps the most pertinent question that comes to mind here is whether or not this "already-recorded" "revealed Word" is to be understood as including the detailed instructions and warnings found in the Spirit of Prophecy. Why is that important?

One thing is certain: Those Seventh-day Adventists who take their stand under Satan's banner will first give up their faith in the warnings and reproofs contained in the Testimonies of God's Spirit.[202]

A final point of illumination on the *iFollow* lessons may be worthy of notice. In October of 2010, *Spectrum* magazine published an interview with "*iFollow's* General Editor, Monte Sahlin."[203] The interview, conducted by Rachel Davies, is informative, giving a good overview of the perceived need for the lessons, as well as the process by which they were developed. Anyone interested in these points would be well served by reading the article.

Beyond the formal material, however, there is interest as well in the reader comments which follow the article. This is the sort of thing that postmodern media users have come to expect, a public forum for the exchange of perceptions. Of course there is a danger in this: this is where the "unwashed masses" get to speak.

Within the first two weeks after publication, the following exchange had taken place between readers with the user names of "Brenda," "James V," and "Monte":

Brenda—From what I have read *iFollow* is an attempt to re-define traditional Adventist doctrines. Even though it is really

---

200 *Spiritual Disciplines: Meditation*, 9; 216.122.106.61/resource.aspx?id=2836&chk=159417410

201 *Spiritual Disciplines: Meditation*, 10; 216.122.106.61/resource.aspx?id=2836&chk=159417410

202 *Selected Messages*, Book Three, 84

203 spectrummagazine.org/node/2721

written with [an] Adventist reader in mind, anyone who has ever read anything from the authors and theologians like Brian McLaren, Richard Foster, Tony Jones, Marcus Borg or N.T. Wright will recognize the ideas and direction. They are heavily quoted and pointed to as additional resources. That is specifically evident in parts about eschatology, faith and doubt, salvation, spiritual disciplines, etc. It will probably be useful to pastors who want to take their churches towards "emerging" conversation. I can't say that Center for Creative Ministries have been very original but it has certainly been creative.

James V—I respect Monte Sahlin's innovation and creative efforts in incorporating these ideas but I am wary since some of these innovations are coming from non-SDA resources, which is allied with "emerging churches"... laced with teachings adapted from spiritualistic "new age" paradigm. We have the Bible and Spirit of Prophecy books... aren't those enough?

Monte—James, I can assure you that we edited out anything that was not rooted in Scripture and the Adventist heritage. There is nothing "New Age" or "spiritualistic" in these materials, not a single jot nor tittle!!

Brenda, there is no attempt in this resource to change anything about Adventist doctrines. That is simply not true!! We teach the same message that the Remnant Church has taught adhering fully to the 28 Fundamentals.

"Brenda" posted twice more to the discussion, at considerable length. As is common in such settings, the writer economized on words, coming up somewhat short of the "full and complete sentences" required back in elementary school. We won't reproduce the entirety of her comments here, but a few selections may be of value:

My intention is not to argue here what's right or wrong, but to point out why I think some lectures are not based on 28 fundamentals and Adventist heritage. Here is an example.

In the lesson *Why Would I Want to Be Saved* theologian cited few times is Marcus Borg, and his book *The Heart of Christianity* is listed as number one resource for further study on the topic. But Borg is not just cited in a sentence or two, in fact the whole lesson is based on the ninth chapter of the mentioned book. ...

After quoting Marcus Borg at some length from a Christian website, Borg's own website, and an interview found on the PBS website, "Brenda" summarizes her perplexity:

Therefore, I really don't understand how does theology about desire or need for salvation from someone who is agnostic about any kind of afterlife, does not believe in deity of Jesus and His material resurrection, or the substitutionary atonement, in any way represents the doctrine of Adventist Church expressed in fundamental beliefs 9 and 10. ...

The whole first section, under the name *Experiencing Spirituality*, meant for those not yet decided to follow Jesus,... is rooted in sources close to those who are embracing emerging vision. Therefore, that means that we are directing them towards this new paradigm. I guess idea is that when they mature spiritually we will point them back towards more traditional Biblical doctrines explained in other sections???

If *iFollow* is not redefining anything, maybe it is redirecting those who decide to follow. [204]

It would have been helpful to read an informed response from someone who knew the *iFollow* materials well, but none was given.

---

204 spectrummagazine.org/node/2721

Chapter Fourteen
Back to Now

THE last three chapters have essentially served the purpose of showing that the influences of the emerging church, meditative or contemplative spirituality, and the whole scope of modern mysticism have been offered to Adventism. What has been covered is certainly not exhaustive, nor has it been particularly hidden from view—but then, in the days of Google, what *is* hidden from view?

More diligent searching through traditional investigative techniques, or even just a few more minutes poking around on the Internet, may well have turned up even more significant institutions and influences. Others may take that time and make that effort if they wish.

The examples cited here have not been pointed out as enemies to be fought nor foes to be destroyed. Though it is theoretically possible, of course, there is no necessity to conclude that the individuals named have acted out of malice against God's church. Remember the story of Dr. David Paulson.[205]

Have mistakes been made? That would be hard to deny. But has God abandoned His people? Has probation closed? Have we been appointed to serve as the judge of the earth? Parallels between the time of Kellogg's Alpha apostasy and the present exist in more areas than simply in what we might point to as heresy.

> All the revelations of the past bring added responsibilities upon the workers in these last days. The past, present, and future are linked together. We must learn lessons from the experiences of other ages. [206]

---

205 See chapters one and two, where Paulson was deeply enmeshed in Kellogg's errors, even arguing with the General Conference president to his face in favor of *The Living Temple*, but was later brought around through the persistent effort of Ellen White. His many years of very profitable work for the Seventh-day Adventist church in the years afterward—not to mention his soul and those of all he worked to save—were the reward won because she refused to give up on the man.

206 *Review and Herald*, July 23, 1895

If there is any one lesson that may be more needed than another, it is that when we see mistakes made, even when we see heresy and apostasy as bad as Dr. Kellogg's, we are still to be our brother's keeper. History tells us clearly that mistakes made in dealing with the Kellogg situation harmed the church—in fact, they "placed on our churches the worst evil that can be placed there."[207]

Often, those who espouse diametrically opposite views—even if they are wrong—can yet be of great value in pointing out the weaknesses of our own positions. Wisdom and humility both argue that we ignore opposing views at our peril, and to deny what is obviously true because it was said by someone from the "other side" is both foolish and wicked.

These lessons apply with full force to many aspects of our discussion, because, sad to say, the advocates of emerging church methods are largely accurate in their diagnoses of the church's current state. Far too many Adventists do live listless, apathetic, spiritless lives, and there is little in such an experience that younger members of the church—let alone the unchurched—will find attractive. To complete the task the Lord has given us will require something other than what we have used in recent decades.

> New methods must be introduced. God's people must awake to the necessities of the time in which they are living. God has men whom He will call into His service—men who will not carry forward the work in the lifeless way in which it has been carried forward in the past. …
>
> In our large cities the message is to go forth as a lamp that burneth. God will raise up laborers for this work, and His angels will go before them. Let no one hinder these men of God's appointment. Forbid them not. God has given them their work. Let the message be given with so much power that the hearers shall be convinced.[208]

All who voice concern with what they see as errors on the part of others within the church, should make sure that "concern" is not

---

207 *Medical Ministry*, 241; see also *d'Sozo: Reversing the Worst Evil*, available from Remnant Publications.

208 *Review and Herald*, September 30, 1902

their only contribution. There is plenty of darkness to accommodate many more lit candles!

Four chapters back we asked, What is the relation of the One Project to the church? That question has been only superficially considered, but we have seen enough to know that the organization certainly did not arise out of a vacuum. Whether the men who met in that Denver hotel knew it or not, they were building on the foundation laid by of others who had gone before them.

But it is the One Project which at the moment seems poised to exert the most obvious influence on God's church. In theory at least, there is a great deal which it espouses to which all should be able to say, Amen! A renewed emphasis on Jesus within the Seventh-day Adventist church is hardly a bad thing. A radical acceptance of His call to discipleship is long overdue. A casting off of those things which have absorbed our time and resources is certainly worth advocating.

So let us be cautious and wise; in Kellogg's case, several fine babies were thrown out with the bath water, and we have nothing to gain by repeating the mistake.

Nor, however, do we have anything to gain by failing to heed the counsel of the Spirit of Prophecy that "the Omega will follow, and will be received by those who are not willing to heed the warning God has given." [209]

What was the warning?

At its simplest, it was basically this:

> In *Living Temple* the assertion is made that God is in the flower, in the leaf, in the sinner. But God does not live in the sinner. The Word declares that He abides only in the hearts of those who love Him and do righteousness. God does not abide in the heart of the sinner; it is the enemy who abides there. [210]

It is an obvious point of concern, then, to see that emerging church ideas tend so commonly to converge on the "contemplative," the "meditative," and the "mystical"—all of which serve as doorways to the overpowering thrill of feeling oneself as one with all creation and possessing inherent divinity. It may be a coincidence … but that wouldn't make it any less deadly!

---

209 *Selected Messages*, Book One, 200

210 *Sermons and Talks*, vol. 1, 343

Chapter Fifteen
In the Limelight

W HAT began as a meeting of friends in a hotel room has grown. The first large "gathering" took place in Atlanta, Georgia, in February 2011, with 172 attendees—friends, family, co-workers, and acquaintances of the founders. In November that same year, the second gathering met in Finland. The following year, 2012, meetings were held in Seattle, Washington; Sydney, Australia; and Copenhagen, Denmark. The schedule for 2013 was Chicago, Illinois; Mjondalen, Norway; Newcastle, Australia; and Newbold College, England. Carrying on, we have Seattle, Sydney, Perth, Utrecht, La Sierra University, and Auckland in 2014, and a special session for 14- to 17-year-olds in 2015.

This is not casual growth, nor is the focus and intent of the organization at all haphazard. Simply navigating the multiple levels of denominational bureaucracy is a formidable challenge that implies strong support by influential individuals. What are they supporting? There is a solid core of philosophical goals within this movement, and the intent is to change the church. Alex Bryan stated it succinctly:

> We need 18- to 22-year-olds trained so that *23- to 35-year-olds* can start *leading* the church. Right away. Then. Now. We need pastorates, pulpits, committees, boards, and initiatives *filled* with *very young* adults. Not tokens. Not the one 27-year-old who is really a 77-year-old in a 20-something body. We need holy and hungry, spiritual and sassy, Christ-centered and creative young people. We need the kind who know a lot about the Bible and the culture. We need those who are friends of Jesus and who can easily make friends with those outside the church. A "piece of the pie" was okay in 1990. But times have changed, for the worse. Now we must give them the *keys to the*

bakery before we have to put a going-out-of-business sign on the window.[211]

The interest expressed in the youth of the church is no pretense. Perhaps the best evidence of the group's interest is the effort they have put forth to reach Adventist teens of high school age. We find the story on the website for a One Project spin-off called the One Life:

> In February 2011, Adventists from all over the globe converged in Atlanta to be part of the One Project: a three-day gathering where each member shared their hopes, dreams, and understandings of Jesus with each other. The One Project was an incredible success as attendees left renewed and hopeful with their eyes set on Jesus. About a month later, a group of teachers and pastors from Southern California began wondering if they could share this singular focus on Jesus with high school students. These teachers and pastors wanted more than anything else to create an environment for an unforgettable encounter with Jesus. From those meetings, the plans were laid for the first ever One Life.
>
> Since August 2011, the One Life experience has been creating space for teenagers to fall in love with Jesus.[212]

Again we see an impressive ability to navigate the complexities of inter-organizational relations. For a self-organized group of "teachers and pastors" to arrange for the use of a conference summer camp, put together an overall program of speakers and activities, and manage the logistics of food and lodging for an unknown number of teenage attendees—and get the necessary permission for all this—between March and August is quite a feat.

This may be partially attributable to experience. Tim Gillespie, Sam Leonor, and Terry Swenson of the One Project have all been integrally involved in the One Life meetings. On the other hand, the

---

211 *Adventist Today*, Winter 2009, 10; this issue is not currently available on the Adventist Today PDF Archive page. It is available through the following site: web.archive.org/web/20111228073635/http://www.atoday.org/issue_pdf. php?pdf=2009-01.pdf

212 the1life.com/about.html

program's success has certainly not been due to publicity in the Pacific Union Conference *Recorder*. There hasn't been a single mention of the One Life program in the nearly three years since it began, at least not in the *Recorder's* pages.

How can that be? How can a weekend program charging $110 for the three day, two night event succeed without any advertising? How is the word getting out? And haven't the *Recorder's* news reporters been missing the story? Surely there must be something of interest going on at these meetings that would deserve coverage. ... There are lots of pictures available on the website,[213] but none in the Union paper.[214]

Perhaps the low public profile aspect of the teen-targeting spin-off enterprise is something the founders of the One Project wish they had tried from the beginning. There is no arguing that the original endeavor has enjoyed considerable publicity, which has fueled its rapid growth in both simple numbers and geographical reach. But growth like that soon produces prominence, prominence increases familiarity, and familiarity results in opinions.

As any public figure knows, other people's opinions can be a tricky thing—especially when those opinions play a role in the decisions made by groups, organizations, or society at large. The classic situation is the selection of someone to fill a public position. Then, because of the importance of the position, and because of the opinions that others hold, the nominee's whole life—words, work, play, etc.—comes under scrutiny. Probably no one enjoys the thought of losing their privacy, but that's why we recognize a difference between "public" and "private." It's a simple reality of life, and it's not going to change any time soon.

And thus it proved in 2012 when one of the One Project founders was nominated for the position of president of Walla Walla University. Alex Bryan, then the senior pastor of the Walla Walla University Church, became the focal point of considerable discussion, spanning the whole range from strong criticism to unwavering defense.

---

213 the1life.com/photos.html

214 More recently, the effort to engage a younger audience has expanded with the announcement of "Generation One 2015," a two-day "gathering, focusing on 14–17-year-olds," and "TOP Kids,… a purposely designed active, creative, responsive experience for… kids aged 2–16 years." the1project.org/gatherings/generation-one-2015; the1project.org/gatherings/sydney-2014

We can only assume the experience was quite unpleasant, and the focus on his past must have felt like an invasion of his privacy. But for those with an interest in the outcome of the talent search, the issues of Bryan's past were the best indicators of the future. Due diligence was called for in an issue as important as a university presidency—what else could they do but consider the past?

And therein lay the concerns. The more-or-less indisputable, credibly reported facts are these:

- **1993**—Alex Bryan became an associate youth pastor at Collegedale [Seventh-day Adventist Church] August 1.[215]

- **1995**—In September 1995, [Alex] Bryan, then a student at the Adventist Theological Seminar at Andrews University, approached Gordon Bietz, president of the Georgia-Cumberland Conference, with his dream of starting a new kind of church—a church that grabbed people's attention. Bietz shared such a dream. ...

- The new church, named the New Community, will target the secular people of Generation X (the generation that follows the baby boomers). ...

- Bryan, the 26-year-old pastor, plans to incorporate multimedia, contemporary music, and dramatic arts to build a worship service that is very creative and authentic. ...

- "The big thing is we've got to allow the language of our generation," says Bryan, who credits many of his ideas to leadership seminars he attended at Willow Creek Community Church,[216] a nondenominational church in northern Chicago. ...

- The leadership team members are all in their 20s—still in college, some finishing master's degrees, others in the workforce.[217]

---

215 *Southern Tidings*, September 1993, 21; docs.adventistarchives.org/docs/SUW/ SUW19930901-V87-09__B/index.djvu?djvuopts&page=21

216 See page 87

217 *Adventist Review*, February 20, 1997, 13; docs.adventistarchives.org/docs/RH/ RH19970220-V174-08__C.pdf

- **1996**—[Alex] Bryan led an evangelistic initiative in Atlanta in 1996, the New Community Fellowship, aimed at reaching secular young adults with the Gospel.[218]

- **2002**—Bryan... resigned in 2002 following disagreements with his employer, the Georgia-Cumberland Conference, over how to most effectively reach unbelievers in the Atlanta area. Bryan's church plant, New Community Church, spent part of Sabbath mentoring inner-city children and renovating a homeless shelter. It also added a worship service on Sunday morning.[219]

- **2007**—On December 1, following months of dialogue, Bryan returned to employment in the same conference. Bryan said he felt an increasing conviction to minister again within the Adventist Church—and cited his renewed appreciation for Adventist doctrines, such as Sabbath rest and the rejection of eternal torment in hell. ...

  Bryan will serve as pastor for mission and ministry at the Collegedale, Tennessee, church. Following the decision of the Conference Executive Committee to employ Bryan, the Church Board voted by a 16–14 margin to affirm the decision.[220]

- **2008**—Alex is currently in the midst of a doctor of ministry program at George Fox University, where he is studying "Leadership in the Emerging Culture." Alex blogs [for *Adventist Today*] on the missional church, emerging cultures, and discipleship from a postmodern perspective.[221]

- **2009**—Alex Bryan... join[ed] the [Walla Walla] University Church [as pastor] in 2009.[222]

---

218 *Southern Tidings*, December 2007, 13; docs.adventistarchives.org/docs/SUW/
SUW20071201-V101-12_C.pdf

219 *Adventist Today*, Jan.–Feb. 2008, 8; atoday.org/issue_pdf.php?pdf=2008-01.pdf

220 *Adventist Today*, Jan.–Feb. 2008, 8; atoday.org/issue_pdf.php?pdf=2008-01.pdf.
In a denomination which quite routinely operates with a considerable degree of consensus on such decisions, a 47% / 53% split is rather unusual.

221 *Adventist Today*, July–Aug. 2008, 6; atoday.org/issue_pdf.php?pdf=2008-04.pdf

222 wwuchurch.org/article/75/about-us/pastors/alex-bio

- **2012**—[On June 15] the Walla Walla University Presidential Search Committee has voted to recommend Alex Bryan to the WWU Board of Trustees as the selected nominee for president of WWU.

  Bryan currently serves as senior pastor of the Walla Walla University Church and has affirmed his willingness to serve as WWU's 24th president.[223]

- Out of a possible 29 members of the [WWU] Board, 25 were present at the July 1 meeting, significantly more than the 15-member quorum required for an official vote. The final vote on the motion to approve Pastor Bryan's name [for the position of president of Walla Walla University] was 9 in favor and 16 against.[224]

Admittedly, this is only an outline of events, but given the sensitive circumstances surrounding some of them, it should be no surprise that fully detailed accounts have not been published. But published accounts aren't the only sources to be considered when hiring a university president, and some individuals with personal knowledge of certain aspects of the case were concerned. That other individuals reacted more to second-hand and even third-hand evidence is entirely likely. But who's to say that anyone should be limited to personal, first-hand knowledge? That's what Thomas demanded, and it earned him a mild—but very direct—rebuke.

Everyone who lives with any sense of community develops a network of trust and respect; when someone you trust tells you something, the default response is to believe that their account is basically true and accurate. If not, you didn't have much trust in the first place! This is normal human procedure, and it works that way for everyone, no matter what political, racial, religious, social, or economic label fits you best. To pretend that only the "other side" of any given issue is "guilty" of this is pure hubris.

To pretend that this process doesn't commonly deteriorate to the level of rumor mongering is just as foolish. Indeed, we live among and work with others just as fallible as ourselves, and it's good to keep a humble and realistic perspective in such matters.

---

223 spectrummagazine.org/blog/2012/06/15/
     walla-walla-univ-search-committee-recommends-pastor-alex-bryan-president

224 spectrummagazine.org/node/4602

Those considering the idea of Pastor Bryan's taking the position of university president had little recourse other than turning to these events of the past to inform themselves of the likely result of his heading up the institution. Just as we can see today, two major features stood out: the large gaps in the above account. What happened between 1996 and 2002? What happened between 2002 and 2007? And, did any of that matter as to the direction Walla Walla University might go under a Bryan presidency?

Shortly before the board's final decision, what has been referred to as the "anonymous letter" made its appearance. *Spectrum* magazine told the story:

> The Walla Walla Union-Bulletin announced Tuesday that John McVay, who stepped down as president of Walla Walla University president in July, has been appointed to serve another term. After six years at the helm of the university, McVay had planned to transition from the president's office to the school of religion where he would teach New Testament studies. However, replacing McVay proved harder than anybody expected.
>
> In June, the presidential search committee recommended Walla Walla University Church senior pastor Alex Bryan as McVay's successor, and the recommendation seemed all but certain to be approved by the university board. However, the certainty of Bryan's approval turned out to be anything but.
>
> An anonymous Internet group started an opposition campaign, citing Bryan's involvement in "Spiritual Formation" as a reason he should not serve as president. The group published a letter of concern[225] online, asking people to contact board chair and North Pacific Union Conference president Max Torkelsen, along with other board members. The offensive proved startlingly effective. Bryan had already been notified of the committee's recommendation and had accepted the call. But the board's vote, generally a formality, came out against him.

---

225 *Spectrum* gives the URL as scribd.com/doc/99744647/
Concerns-Regarding-Alex-Bryan-as-the-New-President-of-Wwu

Torkelsen issued a statement on Bryan's rejection in attempts to quash fast-moving rumors that the university pastor had been lampooned by another web-based witch hunt. Minimizing the role of the anonymous letter and its critique of Bryan's perceived religious qualifications (or disqualifications), Torkelsen pointed to Bryan's lack of educational administrative experience as the reason he was rejected. Torkelsen pushed back against the perception of "undue and unjustified political pressures at work in this process."[226]

Within the academic circles of the church, the news of the final vote was quite commonly decried as an unjustified concession to those who distributed the letter or agreed with its concerns. There is a certain irony in this, since the initial reaction of this same class to Bryan's selection by the presidential search committee had been far from favorable. The idea of a pastor heading an institution of higher learning struck many as a less than convincingly good idea. As one of the first to comment on the announcement put it:

I noted very carefully his qualifications, academics all religion/theology related; employment history church pastor both locally and in a college church setting. Where is his experience in human or organizational leadership? Where is his experience in higher education at any level? I would hate to think this was the best candidate for the position. Walla Walla is not a Bible college for heaven's sake, it is a university. The article announcing his appointment [is] at no point convincing that he was suited to be a university president by today's standards. Leave it to the SDA church to do things differently. These are the appointments that frustrate the real higher education leaders and academicians.[227]

The whole thread of reader comments is actually quite interesting for the picture it paints, both of Pastor Bryan and the *Spectrum* user base. Very quickly there developed two perspectives: a concern

---

226 spectrummagazine.org/node/4672

227 spectrummagazine.org/blog/2012/06/15/
walla-walla-univ-search-committee-recommends-pastor-alex-bryan-president

that the candidate's academic qualifications might not be appropriate (as in the comment above), and a concern that the candidate's spiritual base might not be suitable (as in the comment below):

> I don't quite understand how in less than ten years a pastor who leads a breakaway church is rehabilitated to this extent. Surely there is another more qualified person that the search committee has overlooked. [228]

In other words, the basic concerns later expressed in the anonymous letter were posted on the *Spectrum* website in short order. This is not to say that the readers' comments carried the same tone or intent as did the letter, simply that the facts of the case only supported so many lines of consideration, and intelligent minds were bound to be asking similar questions.

The letter itself claimed to represent the views of "a group of constituents, alumni, educators, pastors, church members, medical professionals, students, and parents." It would be interesting to know more of the make-up of this group, and their reasons for publishing their concerns anonymously. Were they fearful of retaliation? This seems to be a likely factor, for surely some of that group were church employees. The concerns they presented certainly did have an element of opinion (as most value judgments do), but there was substantial evidence presented as well, upon which their opinions were founded. True enough, others might form different opinions from the same evidence, but that's what we call individuality.

In any case, the effect of the letter is uncertain. Did it change the outcome of the board's considerations? North Pacific Union Conference president Max Torkelsen said it did not. Some believed him, some did not.

One thing the letter and the whole turn of events did do—as noted briefly in the *Spectrum* article above—was bring the question of spiritual formation and related concepts to the attention of many minds. Though we will not be considering those specific concerns here, the story we have looked at is of importance for other reasons.

As for Pastor Bryan, the chance to serve as a college president was not lost. Less than a year later—though with far less preliminary

---

228 spectrummagazine.org/blog/2012/06/15/
walla-walla-univ-search-committee-recommends-pastor-alex-bryan-president

notice than in the former instance—the following announcement was made.

> Kettering, Ohio (April 18) – Alex Bryan, D.Min., has been named the sixth president of Kettering College, effective June 1, 2013. He replaces Charles Scriven, Ph.D., who retires this spring after a 12-year tenure at the college. [229]

Those who may have been puzzled as to how all this came about, were even more surprised—and less informed of the decision making process—a few months later when they learned that Pastor Bryan would only serve one year in that capacity.

> Just over six months after leaving as senior pastor of Walla Walla University Church and relocating to Kettering College as the school's sixth president, Alex Bryan has announced that he is leaving—and going back to his old job. …

Walla Walla University Church had not yet named a replacement for Bryan. Walla Walla Church's search committee had been hard at work, and had extended an invitation to Sam Leonor at La Sierra, but had been turned down. Watchers had been expecting an announcement, but Bryan's return comes as a big surprise to many. [230]

---

229 kc.edu/news-room-articles/
     alex-bryan-named-president-of-kettering-college?contentid=8478

230 spectrummagazine.org/blog/2013/12/13/
     alex-bryan-leave-kettering-presidency-and-return-walla-walla

Chapter Sixteen
Gutenberg Lives!

LEONARD Sweet told the students in the Loma Linda University chapel service that the "Gutenberg world" he had been born into had passed away. Books were over. Humanity could be divided into "BC" and "AC"—before and after computers.[231] There is some truth to that. Computers have certainly changed our access to information, but it wouldn't be too hard to argue that books are far from dead.

It's actually a little strange that someone who has written more than forty books—and consistently releases new ones at an impressive rate—would declare them a thing of the past. It's true that the website plays a role somewhat akin to that played by books, but there are differences. The inclusion of audio and video have certainly enhanced the range of data that can be shared, but books still have a niche in the market.

In our topic of interest just now, both books and more modern media provide significant information on the matters at hand. In the last chapter, we discussed the anonymous letter and its purported (and disputed) impact on the WWU presidency search. As it turns out, the letter itself is an interesting element of the story. The fact that it was circulated anonymously may have limited its influence. It was certainly criticized quite broadly on that account. But then—as already mentioned—perhaps the collaborators felt it necessary to sacrifice the moral high ground in exchange for their jobs. Who knows?

But if the letter's impact (whether large or small) wasn't due to the credibility of names attached, it leaves us with the question of how it managed to play any significant role. The answer would seem to be *content*.

Fairness would hasten to add, of course, that even inaccurate content can exert a powerful influence, hence the need for discernment.

---

231 youtube.com/watch?v=He-uUyKhQ6U

Thus, while the letter seems to have been an influence in our story, and the issues it raised are significant, we won't be going through the letter itself. Remember, we're restricting ourselves to "reputable sources," and "Anonymous" doesn't qualify.

It is clear that Pastor Bryan's work at the New Community Church, both before and after he left denominational employment, was a source of concern to many, including both those who wrote the anonymous letter and those who commented on the *Spectrum* website. But what actually happened there while Alex Bryan was the pastor? We've already seen that:

> Bryan, the 26-year-old pastor, plans to incorporate multimedia, contemporary music, and dramatic arts to build a worship service that is very creative and authentic.

> "The big thing is we've got to allow the language of our generation," says Bryan, who credits many of his ideas to leadership seminars he attended at Willow Creek Community Church, a nondenominational church in northern Chicago. [232]

The reference to "multimedia, contemporary music, and dramatic arts" is best understood in light of the subsequent nod to Willow Creek. For anyone not aware, Willow Creek is a megachurch that many Christians and some Adventists have considered a model from which to learn more effective methods. Their taste in "multimedia, contemporary music, and dramatic arts" ranges anywhere from sentimental to dramatic, often rhythmic and loud, and ranging from neo-classical to folk to jazz to rock. [233]

Adventist Today's coverage of the situation implies that there may have been concerns over the church's approach to the Sabbath:

> Bryan ... resigned in 2002 following disagreements with his employer, the Georgia-Cumberland Conference, over how to most effectively reach unbelievers in the Atlanta area. Bryan's

---

232 *Adventist Review*, February 20, 1997, 13; docs.adventistarchives.org/docs/RH/ RH19970220-V174-08__C.pdf

233 Again, youtube.com is the go-to resource. To see the range, try youtube.com/ results?search_query=willow+creek+church+music&sm=3; for a particular example which is not so loud, but in which it's difficult to find anything appropriate for a worship service, see youtube.com/watch?v=_o6UGRIpxpg

church plant, New Community Church, spent part of Sabbath mentoring inner-city children and renovating a homeless shelter. It also added a worship service on Sunday morning. [234]

Sadly, the New Community Church, now pastored by David Bryan, Alex's brother, meets only on Sundays now.[235]

Another characteristic which one might presume was a part of Alex Bryan's pastoral approach is an emphasis on sports. While still employed as an Adventist pastor at the church in Atlanta, Bryan wrote an article for the *Adventist Review*, titled "God and Sports: Can we cheer for Christ on Saturday and Deion Sanders on Sunday?" His closing statement is instructive:

God and sports? Yes. If He is in the arena. [236]

This article illustrates an underlying perspective of the emerging church movement: Nothing is wrong, per se; all elements of culture can and *should be* "claimed for God." This includes not only professional sports, but all forms of music, business, entertainment, media, academia, fashion, etc. In a letter Bryan wrote to the editor of the *Adventist Review* a few years later, we see a similar concept:

Knott's prophetic urging that we might "reclaim the library" (for and with God) should be shared with collegians far and wide. The rich tradition of Adventist education has always drawn on sources far and wide—for God's voice is not easily bound

---

234 *Adventist Today*, Jan.–Feb. 2008, 8; atoday.org/issue_pdf.php?pdf=2008-01.pdf

235 thenewcommunitychurch.com

236 *Adventist Review*, June 21, 2001, 16; archives.adventistreview.org/issue_pdf. php?issue=1525-2001. At any rate, sports is a significant aspect of the current program at the New Community Church. A quick read through the "News" listings on the New Community Church website shows a fondness for sports. "On Saturday, October 19, [2013,] over 100 of us gathered for a night of pumpkin carving, hot chili, CornHole, College football on the outdoor TV, live bluegrass music, S'mores over an open fire, and dozens of pies. On Sunday morning, October 20, we continued our teaching series. ... And then late Sunday night we gathered at a nearby Taco Mac for the Denver-Indianapolis Sunday Night Football showdown! What a weekend!"

"Last Sunday [September 9, 2013] was a day that will forever be remembered at our church. ... [After church] at 12:15, over forty kids spent almost four hours sliding down the mega water-slide (about 880 runs in all!), while others watched football on our big screens, while still others enjoyed fellowship on The Porch over Rick Whalen and his team's amazing BBQ feast!"

(Ps. 19:1–4). Perhaps the school song for the whole of the Adventist school system should be the old hymn "This Is My Father's World"—a confession of God as Creator; a claiming of this earth as His revelation.[237]

Note that "reclaiming the library" is tied to the use of "sources far and wide," i.e., non-Adventist authors. One might wonder who all Pastor Bryan would include in this... if the question hadn't been answered already.

Soon the matter of recommended authors became a major concern. Someone evidently thought that Pastor Bryan's Internet blog might provide insight into the mind of the man who seemed set to lead the institution. A blog, after all, is a public document, and most bloggers are happy to have someone take an interest in what they've posted.

Bryan's blog, though, proved to be quite divisive. The issue was recommended books.[238] Specifically, books from authors with a strong mystical leaning, including *Eat This Book,*[239] and *The Jesus Way,* by Eugene Peterson.[240] *Velvet Elvis,* by Rob Bell.[241] *A Generous*

---

237 *Adventist Review*, April 18, 2013; adventistreview.org/assets/public/ issues/9131511/9131511.pdf

238 Alex Bryan's blog was breakfastfires.blogspot.com, but these recommendations were reportedly deleted after they became a point of contention, and eventually the blog was completely closed out. The name and internet address have since been "resurrected" by someone who apparently has no relation to any of the people or issues dealt with in this book. However, one may see an "internet archive capture" of Pastor Bryan's blog as it appeared on July 25, 2012, at web. archive.org/web/20120726025330/http://breakfastfires.blogspot.com. The book recommendations appear along the right margin of the lower half of the page.

239 In his preface, the author describes this book as "an extended conversation in the practice of spiritual reading," aka, *lectio divina*. Publishers Weekly says, "Peterson recommends a type of Bible-based prayer called *lectio divina*, in which the person praying meditates on a short passage of Scripture and listens for God to speak through the text. Peterson's exposition of lectio divina is one of the fullest to appear in recent years." amazon.com/Eat-This-Book-Conversation-Spiritual/dp/ product-description/0802864902/ref=dp_proddesc

240 See footnote on page 113–114.

241 Rob Bell, though not discussed at any length in this book, is one who may stir the compassion of Seventh-day Adventists. He has been criticized harshly within evangelical circles for expressing reservations about the doctrine of eternal torment. Some say he is a Universalist, others say that he is vague enough in his statements that it's impossible to say what he believes. A similar situation existed for some time

Orthodoxy,[242] by Brian McLaren. *Simply Jesus*, by N.T. Wright. *Jesus Manifesto*, by Leonard Sweet.[243]

It should be obvious that not all these books are going to be equally concerning. Despite the comment that Nouwen's books "all say the same thing,"[244] most authors can't get away with that. Re-runs on TV are one thing, but it doesn't work so well with books. And it should be no surprise to find some really good points made in these books; after all, these authors are generally quite intelligent.

But there are some constants in this: these are all authors who have advocated for emergent ideas and mystical practices—either in these books or in the past; and none of them are blessed with an understanding of the great controversy. They are walking on treacherous ground, without the benefit of the background understanding God has given the Adventist Church. This does not make them enemies, but it does make it dangerous to accept them as instructors or role models.

This is why a warning, a disclaimer, some legal-like fine print at least—something to the extent that there are some aspects of the books or of the author's broader thinking that are not included in the recommendation—would be comforting to see. But there are none.

And this practice seems to be becoming commonplace. Much like the recommendations for further study in the *iFollow* materials, the One Project has given away books which sometimes seem to go beyond what is officially endorsed or advocated at the gatherings themselves. Two examples of those gift books are *Simply Jesus* by N.T. Wright, and *I am a Follower* by Leonard Sweet.[245] In these cases

---

in regard to his position on homosexuality, but that ambiguity seems to have been settled by these statements:

"I am for marriage. I am for fidelity. I am for love, whether it's a man and a woman, a woman and a woman, a man and a man." "And I think the ship has sailed. This is the world we are living in and we need to affirm people wherever they are." (en. wikipedia.org/wiki/Rob_Bell)

242 Pastor Bryan commented on this volume: "as I finish reading this masterpiece I find myself recommending it again and again. ... this is perhaps the single most important book I've read in the past five years." For more on this book, see the footnote on page 95.

243 See page 89–90.

244 See page 77.

245 See the excerpts from this book on page 93.

it is no longer simply a recommendation without a disclaimer, it has gone a step beyond. And still with no disclaimer, no cautionary note, no disavowal of anything.[246]

One might begin to think they actually believe what they recommend or hand out. … and that raises uncomfortable questions. If they believe it, why wouldn't they teach it themselves? After all, you can't spread ideas without talking about them, can you?

Well, yes, actually you can. That's the reason for Adventist publishing houses. It's what we used to call the "silent preacher," and the idea isn't foreign to at least one of the One Project leaders:

> By reading, people will learn and change and transform their lives. [247]

It is unpleasant even to think that people might be less-than-forthright in representing their intentions. But how far can we stretch the English language? How much contradiction can be attributed to mere "linguistics"? How far apart can human understandings drift solely because of the tendency to see things from different perspectives?

When Leonard Sweet writes, "Let me say first of all that for me, New Age rhymes with sewage,"[248] we *want* to accept it.

When the editor of *iFollow* says "I can assure you that we edited out anything that was not rooted in Scripture and the Adventist heritage. There is nothing 'New Age' or 'spiritualistic' in these materials, not a single jot nor tittle!!"[249] we *want* to believe he means what we think he said.

And when Alex Bryan protests to his union conference president, "I am absolutely opposed to any form of Eastern mysticism,

---

246 In yet another step in this direction, the One Project's 2014 "gathering" in Seattle included a short, live presentation by Leonard Sweet.

247 Japhet De Oliveira, *Adventist Review*, March 15, 2012; archives.adventistreview.org/issue__pdf.php?issue=2012-1508

248 *A Response to Recent Misunderstandings*, leonardsweet.com/download_sad1.php?file=63_Response to Critics.pdf

249 spectrummagazine.org/node/2721; see page 122.

mantras, centering prayer, or other non-Biblical forms of spiritual exercise,"[250] we truly wish we could see it that way.

But it's hard, and it's all the fault of those relics of the Gutenberg era, those printed materials which seem to say so many things opposite or far beyond what the individuals say themselves.

In Leonard Sweet's case, it's his forty-two published books, particularly (but far from exclusively) the unrecanted *Quantum Spirituality*. For the *iFollow* editors, it's the tutorials on meditation, and guided imagery, along with the scores of references to emergent advocates. And for the One Project it's the give away books at their gatherings—again promoting the same emergent authors.

Many would say that we should be more accepting of others' views, and in many cases that might apply. There are issues upon which sincere Christians may see things differently, and in many cases they may all be correct, having simply considered the topic from different angles.

But pantheism *isn't* one of those issues:

In *Living Temple* the assertion is made that God is in the flower, in the leaf, in the sinner. But God does not live in the sinner. The Word declares that He abides only in the hearts of those who love Him and do righteousness. God does not abide in the heart of the sinner; it is the enemy who abides there."[251]

These next statements are even more pointed, given the claims of those engaging in contemplative prayer and the like:

---

250 This statement appears in a letter from Pastor Bryan to Elder Max Torkelsen, apparently written shortly after the anonymous letter gained notoriety. It was available at spiritualformationsda.wordpress.com for some time, but the blog has been converted to a private status requiring a user name and password. See spectrummagazine.org/article/column/2012/07/26/crisis-leadership#comment-599143848. This highlights one of the weak points of the "postmodern" technologies—references change; websites disappear. Fortunately for those interested in piecing together the history of this topic, this document and many others are preserved in a series of PowerPoint presentations available (for now...) at slideshare.net/ronduff. Very thorough documentation from Ron Duffield, a skilled researcher.

251 *Sermons and Talks*, vol. 1, 343

Whatever may be the ecstasies of religious feeling, Jesus cannot abide in the heart that disregards the divine law. God will honor those only who honor Him.[252]

"Not every one that saith unto me, Lord, Lord, shall enter into the kingdom of heaven; but he that doeth the will of my Father which is in heaven"—the will made known in the ten commandments, given in Eden when the morning stars sang together, and all the sons of God shouted for joy, and spoken with an audible voice from Sinai. "Many will say to me in that day, Lord, Lord, have we not prophesied in thy name? and in thy name have cast out devils? and in thy name done many wonderful works? And then will I profess unto them, I never knew you: depart from me, ye that work iniquity." Many mighty works are done under the inspiration of Satan, and these works will be more and more apparent in the last days. [253]

The point is simple: there is a difference between "the faith," and "deceiving spirits and doctrines of demons."[254] This is a difference we would do well to remember.

---

252 *The Sanctified Life*, 92

253 *Review and Herald*, May 7, 1901

254 1 Timothy 4:1

Chapter Seventeen

Chaff-Filled Fields

AS mentioned in previous chapters, there is often seen within the Adventist version of the emergent church teachings, something like a game of "chicken." Those who advocate these ideas seemingly try to get as close to emergent ideas as possible, without ever uttering the words. It's a little like driving at full speed toward a forbidden line, and then slamming on the brakes. The car stops in time, but the passengers fly through the windshield and land on the other side… with a recommended (or freely supplied) handbook of contemplative practices conveniently nearby.

Is this on purpose? Or just an amazing coincidence? Remember, this is in the context of a deadly heresy. It really is important to consider the results of this. And so we include one more story that comes up in Google.

To understand the details of this requires quoting some fairly lengthy context, more than a good editor would normally allow. But it's important that the story make sense, so we will begin with the introduction of a blog site on the Internet.[255]

The blog in question is titled *Reimagining Adventism by Reinventing the Adventist Wheel,* [256] and it offers this "Message for Non-Adventists":

> If you are curious about Adventists in general, this blog may not be for you. It is currently an online magazine that includes general interest articles and YouTube videos. Our religious contributors usually express themselves without reference to traditional Adventist theology. However, if you have an Adventist friend, you might be interested to know that if you scratch the skin, he or she might be more Christian than "Adventist." So, if

---

255 For anyone not familiar with the term, a "blog" is simply a website where one person (the "blogger") writes out thoughts, plans, observations, what have you. To such a "post," others may be allowed to append comments of their own.

256 reinventingsdawheel.blogspot.ca

you decide to check out the progressive, left-leaning, fringe of Christian Adventism, this blog is your opportunity. [257]

One might wonder about this claim to represent "the progressive, left-leaning, fringe of Christian Adventism." It sounds a little bit like a four-year-old boy saying, "I'm a monster!" But take it for what it's worth, and be thankful for the frank admission that "this blog may not be for [everyone]."

Our particular interest begins on a specific page, a post that was put up back in 2007 by a contributor with the user name of Nathan Brown:[258]

Thoughts from a Harry Potter Agnostic:

For the past 10 years, I have been a Harry Potter agnostic. While enjoying the stories as just that—stories—with each installment, I have been aware of their questionable literary merit and frustrated, with the increasing size of the successive volumes, about the seeming absence of a hard-nosed editor from J.K. Rowling's literary life. Even about the 400-page mark of *The Deathly Hallows*, it was more determination to see how it would end than my engagement in the story that kept me reading.

But the greater cause of my Potter agnosticism was the continuing ambiguity about the nature of the story and characters themselves. Having read opinions on the Harry Potter series from across the spectrum, I was unable to settle the question in my mind. Of course, there were the hardline, angry Christian perspectives, who were askance at any mention of wizards and magic in anything less than a completely negative way and—ignoring the use of such motifs as literary devices—were ready to declare Harry the illegitimate son of the antichrist himself. [259]

---

257 reinventingsdawheel.blogspot.ca/p/message-for-non-adventists.html

258 This blogger's profile page may be found at blogger.com/
profile/03546525288795311952

259 This is almost enough to make one wonder if the former magicians of Ephesus could not have seen those expensive books in a different light by simply recognizing their use of "literary devices." See Acts 19:19

On the other hand have been those educators and parents just happy to see kids put down the Playstation controller for a moment and pick up a book, like we did in the "good, old days." And of course there were also Harry Potter's grown-up fans, drawn in by a remarkably readable story.

And then there was one more school of thought of which I had read a little—those Christian voices who were keen to point out the goodness embedded in the Potter stories. Some even went so far as to suggest Rowling—who has always been reticent in talking about issues of faith—was a Christian, using her writing to get "past watchful dragons" (as C.S. Lewis put it) in a post-Christian society, particularly in her native England.

So my anticipation of the seventh and concluding book of the series was heightened more by this underlying ideological tension than by my mere curiosity as to how the story was to end, whether Harry was going to make it out alive, and how neatly Rowling was going to wrap up the loose ends. Without denying my enjoyment of a rollicking narrative, it was more as an observer of a cultural phenomenon that I made the pilgrimage to a suburban bookstore on the Saturday evening of its release and purchased one of the record 12 million copies sold on the day.

So am I a believer? As I have mentioned, two-thirds of the way through *Harry Potter and the Deathly Hallows*, I was still to be convinced. And, in our cynical age, it is remarkably difficult to write an ending that is both credible and satisfying.

But J.K. Rowling pulled it off—and in ways that few of the many speculators were able to predict. As a modern-day fairy tale, the series works, while still giving the literary purists things to grumble about.

And, ideologically, my agnosticism has also faded. A few years back, I was a volunteer at a church teen camp at which the speaker used the early books of the Harry Potter series to explore the themes of the Great Controversy and book 7 brings the battle between good and evil to its climax. This motif has been an important part of the ongoing story—as it is in many of our culture's great stories—and the distinction between good and evil becomes clearer as the characters are forced to choose their response to the growing conflict. While the dark side employ whatever means possible to achieve their ends, the Harry Potter heroes choose to make space for compassion and maintain self-imposed limits on their use of power.

But Rowling also portrays the choice between good and evil as not so black-and-white as one-dimensional stereotypes might be. The good guys have their flaws, doubts and struggles, while some of the worst characters are not beyond moments of ambiguity and even the possibility of redemption, if they choose.

And the central choices are those Harry must make. Does he have faith in Dumbledore's instructions, despite the questions raised about his mentor after Dumbledore's death? And ultimately is Harry prepared to face his own death, trusting that somehow his sacrifice will destroy the evil of Lord Voldemort and put an end to the reign of terror?

In a scene that wakes strong echoes of Aslan's self-sacrifice, his walk to the stone table and his death in Lewis' *The Lion, the Witch and the Wardrobe*, Potter dons the cloak of invisibility for a final trip into the Forbidden Forest to face Voldemort and his minions. And then the "deeper magic"—as Lewis describes it—does its thing. In both Narnia and Harry Potter, love, goodness and humility are stronger than evil, even when evil appears triumphant.

A believer? No, I don't believe in Harry Potter, I have not rushed out to join a HP fan club and I have not sent any money (after my initial "donation" of about $30 for the book itself). But at the end of our 10-year adventure with Harry Potter's fantasy world and J.K. Rowling's roller coaster of a story, I have been reminded of the importance of choosing goodness and trusting that goodness to overcome evil, whatever it might cost and however doubtful it might appear.

As a result of reading Harry Potter, I am encouraged as a believer in God and in His purposes and plan for goodness in a world that often doesn't look like it. And I am hopeful that others who may not yet be as familiar with the realities of the kingdom of God might recognize something of this same self-sacrificing goodness when they hear the story of Jesus and what He has done to overcome the evil in our world.[260]

Following this post, there is a series of eleven comments made in a sort of round robin style going back and forth between five different users. The conversation tends to be mildly anti-Potter in tone, and then somewhat surprisingly turns to "where to find God." In the process, one of the users commented:

God is not in everything and we don't find [Him] anywhere we look in this world... that's pantheism.

To this, the user addressed responded:

I also agree with you that "God is not in everything,..." I was saying—and obviously not very well—that God sometimes speaks in ways, and in places, that seem to be what I felt Shawn was talking about, "cloaked in the garb of error."

After another couple exchanges, the eleventh comment closed with:

That's my problem with this approach, instead of really looking for light and truth in God's sure revelation, why look in places where I'm actually putting my faith at risk? I don't think God works like that, light is not found in the darkness. …

The twelfth comment, dated July 30, 2007, is from Alex Bryan:[261]

---

260 reinventingsdawheel.blogspot.ca/2007/07/thoughts-from-harry-potter-agnostic.html

261 This blogger's profile appears to have been deleted, and is now only available through the web.archive.org site, which shows the page as it appeared on June 30, 2008; web.archive.org/web/20080630041125/blogger.com/profile/17133285432646924270

I would like to affirm Nathan's use of Harry Potter.

1. God is, indeed, in all things. Even chaff-filled fields of wheat. There is great danger in limiting where God can and shall be found.

2. I see Scripture as the "trunk" of a 4,000-year old tree of spiritual stories. Very important. But truth found in flimsier branches may even be MORE important if millions of people are out on this limb!

3. Scripture is not truth. Jesus is truth, and scripture merely speaks of Him. There is a difference. And He shall be revealed in many odd and interesting places. Are there greater revelations than Scripture? Yes. Jesus, for one. And the Holy Spirit, now, for another. Scripture is our "guide" to the Spirit.

4. Finally, of all people, Christians should embrace stories of the spiritual world. Not literally, always. Not orthodoxically, always. But Jesus drew out Satan, drew out demons, drew out evil in order to show the supremacy of The Spirit.

Harry Potter is… an opportunity. Thanks, Nathan.

These comments were not convincing to all, apparently, for a reply came back to challenge this thinking:

Problems with Alex's approach:

1. God is NOT in all things, this is the old Pantheism idea which has been dealt with long ago. Is God in my morning cereal? If not, why not?

2. Can Bible truth be manipulated to fit people's experiences or to be culturally relevant? Does new relevance abolish old relevance? Is relevance universal? This goes along Catholicism's idea that Scripture is only relevant because Priests and Popes make it relevant; tradition (dare we say culture?) supplants the Bible;

3. Scripture reveals Jesus and therefore IS truth. However, can something else that "reveals" Jesus be considered Scripture as well? Would it be authoritative as the Scriptures? If it were possible for Harry Potter to reveal Jesus…, would it be in the same level as Scriptures? What is special about the Scriptures really and why should it continue to be the foundation of our belief instead of all that literary prowess of secular authors?

4. Should Christians really embrace all that is branded as ethereal, transcendent and "spiritual"? Should we ask Lucifer how he used to know God, how he felt before his fall and how heaven is like? Surely he would be an excellent source of information…

Alex Bryan did not respond. Another user suggested an article to read in the *Adventist Review* (but included a link to an issue with nothing on Potter). This was followed by:

What about that little verse in Philippians chapter 4:

"Finally, brothers and sisters, whatever is true, whatever is worthy of respect, whatever is just, whatever is pure, whatever is lovely, whatever is commendable, if something is excellent or praiseworthy, think about these things."

I'm tempted to think Harry Potter fails a good number of these "tests."

And, finally, the page closes with a short statement from a new user, made six-and-a-half years after the others:

Harry Potter rules.

And that, for those who didn't know, is how a blog works.

But what are we to make of Pastor Bryan's comments?

For starters, let's acknowledge that this was written some years ago, about the time he began those "months of dialogue" which culminated in his being rehired by the Georgia-Cumberland Conference as "pastor for mission and ministry at the Collegedale,

Tennessee, church." Just as we said of Leonard Sweet, it isn't fair to judge a man by words he may no longer believe. The fact that Pastor Bryan has deleted his user profile from the site can be interpreted as an indication of some distancing from his activity there.

Secondly, we should recognize that it's possible to interpret his words in more than one way, especially on point number one.

Did he really mean that "God is in all things" the way a full-blown pantheist would mean it?

It's probable that "chaff-filled fields of wheat" is a metaphor for a mixture of error and truth, an allusion to Jeremiah 23:28 ("'What is the chaff to the wheat?' says the Lord"[262]). It's possible to argue that since this comment is metaphorical, the comment that "God is in all things" should be taken metaphorically as well.

That might limit the comment to mean something like "God is in all examples of literature—including those filled with error," but even that position poses problems. First, of course, is the issue of the verse in Jeremiah: its obvious meaning is that the chaff is of no value to those who desire wheat. Do we really want to try defending *all* literature? Is there good to be found in Anton LeVey's *Satanic Bible* (to cite one of the more obviously sensational examples)?

And the idea that "there is great danger in limiting where God can and shall be found," is patently un-Biblical Biblical. Unaided human wisdom would certainly fail to identify where God can be found, but that certainly doesn't prevent an inspired distinction. If that were the case, what could Jesus possibly have meant when He said:

> Then if anyone says to you, "Look, here is the Christ!" or "There!" do not believe it. For false christs and false prophets will rise and show great signs and wonders to deceive, if possible, even the elect. See, I have told you beforehand. Therefore if they say to you, "Look, He is in the desert!" do not go out; or "Look, He is in the inner rooms!" do not believe it.[263]

---

262 Isn't it clear that this verse would argue against paying any attention to Harry Potter in the first place, except perhaps to identify the whole phenomenon as "the illegitimate son of the antichrist himself" if necessary? There is a danger in the liberal passivity which finds all things "good."

263 Matthew 24:23–27. Howard Peth makes a perceptive observation about Matthew 24:5, which says, "For many will come in My name, saying, 'I am the Christ,' and

Interestingly enough, the naïve idea that one can go looking for God anywhere and everywhere isn't even accepted by Richard Foster. In his book *Prayer: Finding the Heart's True Home*, a highly regarded manual on contemplative prayer, Foster writes:

> I also want to give a word of precaution. In the silent contemplation of God we are entering deeply into the spiritual realm, and there is such a thing as supernatural guidance that is not divine guidance. ... There are various orders of spiritual beings, and some of them are definitely not in cooperation with God and His way! [264]

What are we to make of his second comment? If the Bible is the trunk, what are the "flimsier branches" with "millions of people... out on" them? The obvious candidate in this context is the Potter book. If so, is it really advisable to go looking for "even more important" truth to be found there?

His third point ("Scripture is not truth") is hard-edged. Surely Pastor Bryan was familiar with John 17:17. ("Sanctify them by Your truth. Your word is truth.") "Scripture merely speaks of Him," the pastor wrote. Yes, Scripture speaks of Christ—"these are they which testify of Me." [265] But "*merely* speaks"? "All Scripture is given by inspiration of God," [266] and that ought to count for something.

This foreign-to-the-Bible separation between Jesus and Scripture is a key issue, one which returns with the comment that "Scripture is our 'guide' to the Spirit."

Jesus clearly had it turned the other way round—"The Helper, the Holy Spirit, whom the Father will send in My name, He will teach you all things, and bring to your remembrance all things that I said to you." [267]

---

will deceive many." In his book, *The Dangers of Contemplative Prayer*, he points out that only the teachings of inherent divinity could realistically lead to many people claiming to be "the Christ."

264 *Prayer: Finding the Heart's True Home*, 156

265 John 5:39

266 2 Timothy 3:16

267 John 14:26

And if the Holy Spirit is a *"greater* revelation than Scripture,"
does that include the authority to supersede scriptural commands?
Here we see the very heart of the contemplative issue: What is the
relationship between the Incarnate Word and the Inspired Word?

We know they aren't supposed to contradict each other, but the
uniform end result of contemplative, pantheistic, mystical thought
and practice is to subordinate the objective teachings of Scripture to
the leading of the subjectively experienced "divinity," and often an
internal divinity at that.

The concern of this book is that certain publications and practices now being promoted by some within the Adventist church lead
to just that outcome. When the powerful personal experience of "Jesus" leads away from Scripture, we see results reminiscent of Ellen
White's comment:

> As I am shown these special things of Satan's science, and how
> he deceived the holy angels, I am afraid of the men who have
> entered into the study of the science that Satan carried into
> the warfare in heaven. ... How my heart has been agonized as
> I have seen souls accepting the inducements held out to them
> to unite with those who were warring against God. When they
> once accept the bait it seems impossible to break the spell that
> Satan casts over them, because the enemy works out the sci-
> ence of deception as he worked it out in the heavenly courts. [268]

Pastor Bryan's fourth comment, that "of all people, Christians
should embrace stories of the spiritual world," applied to the Harry
Potter book under discussion, is simply... *what*? Wrong? Misguided?
Dangerous? Maybe, "D, all of the above," is the best answer.

Again, as we have already seen in relation to sports and "the library," the underlying principle is that *everything* is acceptable if it is
"claimed for God." But this completely ignores the Biblical injunc-
tion to *stay away* from some things!

---

268 *Manuscript Releases*, vol. 11, 212

You cannot drink the cup of the Lord and the cup of demons; you cannot partake of the Lord's table and of the table of demons. [269]

Therefore "Come out from among them and be separate, says the Lord. Do not touch what is unclean, and I will receive you." [270]

Do not be unequally yoked together with unbelievers. For what fellowship has righteousness with lawlessness? And what communion has light with darkness? [271]

And have no fellowship with the unfruitful works of darkness, but rather expose them. [272]

And I heard another voice from heaven saying, "Come out of her, my people, lest you share in her sins, and lest you receive of her plagues." [273]

And, of course, there is this counsel:

Suffer not yourselves to open the lids of a book that is questionable. There is a hellish fascination in the literature of Satan. It is the powerful battery by which he tears down a simple religious faith. Never feel that you are strong enough to read infidel books; for they contain a poison like that of asps. They can do you no good, and will assuredly do you harm. In reading them, you are inhaling the miasmas of hell. [274]

Some readers may well be wondering by this point about the wisdom of including these stories of one individual's past experience. The story of the New Community Church, the search for a university president, the recommending of "questionable" books,

---

269 1 Corinthians 10:21

270 2 Corinthians 6:17

271 2 Corinthians 6:14

272 Ephesians 5:11

273 Revelation 18:4

274 *Fundamentals of Christian Education*, 93

and someone's opinion of Harry Potter—aside from the common denominator of emergent church perspectives, what has all this to offer?

Primarily this one observation: none of these issues seem to have posed an impediment in terms of a career path within the sphere of Adventism's ministerial and academic circles.

What are the odds of—as the *Spectrum* blogger phrased it—"a pastor who leads a breakaway church... [being] rehabilitated to this extent"? Taken back into employment, not in some humble little rural church on a probationary status, but immediately appointed "pastor for mission and ministry" at the second largest[275] Adventist church in the United States. Nominated to be the president of, not one university, but two. The One Project, of which he was a founding board member, provided support by fifty-four church entities.

None of this shows any negative response to the issues raised in this volume. The implication is obvious: for whatever reasons, and with whatever level of knowledge, many responsible individuals within the denomination's decision making circles apparently have either not considered or find no concern with the principles and practices of the emergent church.

---

275 hirr.hartsem.edu/cgi-bin/mega/
db.pl?db=default&uid=default&view_records=1&ID=*&sb=2

Chapter Eighteen
Suddenly It's Everywhere

ONE of the most puzzling aspects of these emerging church concepts is the apparent speed with which they have spread. To many church members, these ideas and practices seem to be sprouting up overnight like mushrooms all over the lawn. Indeed, the time span in which these developments have been easily seen is quite short.

True, the Leadership Institute began taking pastors on "The Journey" in 1993, but nothing was said about it in the church papers, so the average lay member probably never heard of it. There was some helpful coverage of their programs in *Adventist Today*, but since that magazine is not an official organ of the denomination and has a small circulation when compared to church membership, relatively few rank-and-file believers were aware of it.

The more visible elements we have looked at have all made their entrance into Adventism since 2010. For these to have gained the degree of prominence and influence they have in such a short time is remarkable. How has this happened?

We noted one aspect previously: the founders and board members of the One Project—despite the mysterious vicissitudes of Alex Bryan's employment—are all men and women of influence. Let's look at the list: [276]

- Alex Bryan (One Project Chair), Senior Pastor of the Walla Walla University Church

- Japhet De Oliveira (One Project Chair), Senior Pastor of the Boulder Seventh-day Adventist Church

- Dilys Brooks, Associate Campus Chaplain, Loma Linda University

- Ken Denslow (Ex Officio), Assistant to the President, North American Division

---

276 the1project.org/about/board.html

- Lisa Clark Diller, History Dept. Chair, Southern Adventist University
- David Franklin, Co-host of *Let's Pray!*, Hope Channel
- Tim Gillespie, Faith Community and Health Liaison, Loma Linda University Health
- Sam Leonor, University Chaplain, La Sierra University
- Rod Long, Property Developer and Project Manager
- Paddy McCoy, University Chaplain, Walla Walla University
- Terry Swenson, University Chaplain, Loma Linda University

Clearly this is an accomplished group, filling influential positions mainly within the circles of Adventist academia. Along with these, we might consider some of the more prominent names selected from the larger list of the One Project's "Consultants."[277]

- Tony Anobile: President, Arizona Conference
- Ed Barnett: President, Rocky Mountain Conference
- Chris Blake: Professor of English, Union College
- Phil Brown: President, Newbold College
- Gary Councell: Director, Adventist Chaplains
- Manny Cruz: Associate Youth Director, North American Division
- John Freedman: President, Washington Conference
- Dany Hernandez: Senior Pastor, LifeSource Adventist Fellowship[278]
- Eddie Hypolite: Senior Pastor, Avondale College Church
- Roy Ice: Young Adult Pastor, Loma Linda
- Tony Knight: Youth Director, Australian Union
- Rob Lang: Youth Director, Georgia Cumberland Conference
- Victor Marley: Youth & Family Director, Norwegian Union Conference

---

277 the1project.org/about/consultants.html; unfortunately, space does not allow the listing of all forty-four consultants. No disrespect is intended toward those not included here.

278 Lifesource Adventist Fellowship (Denver, Colorado), may be close to what Pastor Bryan intended at the New Community Church. See vimeo.com/user3626469/videos/page:1/sort:date

- Thomas Muller: President, Danish Union
- Eric Penick: Youth Director, Southeastern California Conference
- Jaci Cress Perrin: Chaplain, Adventist Health System
- Ray Pichette: President, Illinois Conference
- Tommy Poole: Chaplain, Gem State Academy
- Aaron Purkeypile: Associate Treasurer, Washington Conference
- Sandy Roberts: Executive Secretary, Southeastern California Conference[279]
- Ken Rogers: Youth Director, Southern Union Conference
- Garrett Speyer: Youth Pastor, Loma Linda University Church
- Cheonneth Strickland: Youth Director, Sydney Conference
- Erik VanDenburgh: Youth Director, Arizona Conference
- Tracy Wood: Director for Youth Ministry, Oregon Conference

It would be interesting to hear the stories behind each of these relationships. How did these people all come together? Where did they meet? Of the second list above, only Roy Ice's story has been mentioned; he's the drummer for Big Face Grace. Clearly this is the fruit of some extensive Adventist networking, with this group leaning more toward the administrative functions of the church.

The question is hard to avoid: How did all this come about? By happenstance? Really?

It's possible, of course, that all this came about simply because—as Solomon put it—"time and chance happen to them all."[280] But the wisest man who ever lived also said "The hand of the diligent will rule."[281] So which is it in this case? What has led to the rapid spread of "emerging church" concepts, books, and proponents—coincidence or determination?

That is a question for omnipotence to answer confidently, and all others to admit the speculative nature of their thoughts, but there is,

---

279 This listing is given as found on the One Project "Consultants" page. It has obviously not been updated since Roberts' recent election to the position of President of the Southeastern California Conference.

280 Ecclesiastes 9:11

281 Proverbs 12:24

back near the beginning of this story, a most interesting document, one which just may have a bearing on this question.

On the website of the Leadership Institute is a document referred to as the Wilberforce Monograph. Its full title is "The Spirituality and Mission of William Wilberforce and the Clapham Sect."[282] The document is attributed to Paul Jensen, the founder of the Leadership Institute, and is dated November 1999.

In many regards, there is nothing surprising. Jensen quotes Willard, Peterson, Foster, and Brother Lawrence; and, of course, he promotes spiritual formation. But then he tells a story, the biography of William Wilberforce, an English Evangelical who lived from 1759–1833. Wilberforce and about a dozen others who worked with him came to be known as the Clapham Sect.

There is much that Seventh-day Adventists can find to admire in the Clapham Sect, not the least of which was their predominant influence in the struggle which finally led to the abolition of slavery within the British Empire. The story is well worth reading for a number of reasons, but just now we must focus narrowly. A few quotations should be of interest:

> In face of the widespread drunkenness, absenteeism and powerlessness among Anglican clergy at the time, Simeon, Thornton and others determined to fill the Anglican pulpits of the land with Evangelical clergy. How did they do this?
>
> First, various funds were established to help Evangelical university students who wanted to be ordained but lacked the finances to finish their schooling. But training young men for ministry would be of little use if there were no places for them to serve. Therefore, Simeon and Thornton bought the rights to present clergyman to a particular parish or living. These were called advowsons. A living held money in trust from which the interest provided the salary of the clergy who occupied the living. ...
>
> Simeon set up a trust to buy livings for evangelicals and by the time he died in 1836, the Simeon trustees held the advowson of twenty-one livings. Where Evangelicals could not buy

---

282 spiritualleadership.com/wp-content/uploads/2012/04/clapham.pdf

livings, they tried to place Evangelical curates in parishes of non-resident clergy or in parishes where the living was held by a plurality of patrons. This was largely the work of the Church Pastoral Aid Society which was set up in 1836 by Lord Shaftesbury, Wilberforce's successor as the leader of the Evangelical movement. If all else failed, Evangelicals would build a chapel and fill it with Evangelical clergy.

So effective were these and other attempts that the number of evangelical clergy grew from an estimated one in twenty in 1800 to about one in every three by the mid-nineteenth century.[283]

There is much more to the historical account, of course, but let's jump to some of the "lessons and implications" Jensen points out:

> Two ministry insights from the way the Sect worked. ... Structures must be developed or modified, acceptable to the larger body, in which "graduates" can express the ministry/mission for which they were trained. My organization, The Leadership Institute, is doing this presently with our Postmodern Mission Project (which plants churches for the next generations). ... Secondly... wherever possible we should create lay sodalities (mission structures) with spirituality at the center of those structures. Though they may not be initially accepted within existing structures... they will serve a crucial role in expanding and renewing the church.[284]

This might be taken as a case of "wise as serpents, harmless as doves," if it were not for the certainty that the "spirituality" to be established at the center of all these efforts is the contemplative variety which establishes itself as being above Scripture. The truth is, this is *wise as serpents, deadly as serpents*. But let's go on:

Next Jensen points to a "movement towards younger leaders in church and state" as a part of the Clapham success:

---

283 Paul Jensen, *The Spirituality and Mission of William Wilberforce and the Clapham Sect*, 26–27

284 Paul Jensen, *The Spirituality and Mission of William Wilberforce and the Clapham Sect*, 37

King George III ascended to the throne at a young age. Wilberforce was elected to Parliament when he was 21. Pitt became Prime Minister in his early twenties. Simeon also became Vicar at Holy Trinity Church in his early twenties. At a time of momentous change, old leadership was being replaced by a new generation of leadership which was anxious for change. It was a revolutionary period. The new patterns of leadership were crucial to the work of the Sect. ...

[Today], a whole new generation shaped by postmodernism is redefining the church. To those under thirty-five the church is relationships, not institution.[285]

Unfortunately, it often appears that this dismissal of institutions is prone to include the dismissal of Scripture. The practical result is to make *relationship* supreme.

And finally, in discussing the relative lack of academic theologians in the Clapham movement, Jensen sees a contrast in our day:

In our context, God is raising up a generation of Christian scholars whom he is sending as missionaries into the academy. [286]

So what does all this mean? Has Paul Jensen written the master plan that others are following? Is this a conspiracy, or merely a case of like-minded individuals coming to share the same perspective and arriving at similar conclusions?

In one sense, it matters not. We know there is a vast demonic conspiracy, the details of which are painted quite clearly in *The Great Controversy*. It is not necessary for us to know all that transpires on the purely human level. Besides, if Google can't find it, perhaps we don't need to know.

What *is* important is to remember that a greater authority than the Internet has spoken to us. We have been warned.

---

285 Paul Jensen, *The Spirituality and Mission of William Wilberforce and the Clapham Sect*, 38

286 Paul Jensen, *The Spirituality and Mission of William Wilberforce and the Clapham Sect*, 39; In this comment, of course, "academy" is not a reference to a single institution, but to the academic world as a whole.

Chapter Nineteen

Comparison

THE general premise of this book is that present circumstances appear in many ways to be similar to what one might suspect the prophesied Omega apostasy to be like. That is a serious claim, one that should not be made—or accepted—lightly. To evaluate such a claim requires a familiarity with the prophecy itself, and the details of the Alpha apostasy of Kellogg's day. If a refresher is necessary, you might wish to re-read chapters one through seven.

Chapter two identified five major features of the Alpha experience, and these were then expanded on in chapters three through seven. Let's take a quick look at those items, comparing them with what we've seen in the emerging church movement, particularly as it has played out within Adventism.

1. The first characteristic was the subtlety of the error, which resulted in a tragic delay in anyone seeking to correct the problem. Kellogg, and others, had been talking up a somewhat watered down version of pantheism for several years, and no one had raised objection. This was, to Ellen White at least, a huge red flag:

> To me it seems passing strange that some who have been long in the work of God cannot discern the character of the teaching in *Living Temple* in regard to God. [287]

> The sentiments in *Living Temple* regarding the personality of God have been received even by men who have had a long experience in the truth. When such men consent to eat of the fruit of the tree of knowledge of good and evil, we are no longer to regard the subject as a matter to be treated with the greatest delicacy. That those whom we thought sound in the faith should have failed to discern the specious, deadly influence of this science of evil, should alarm us as nothing else has alarmed us.

---

287 *Manuscript Releases*, vol. 11, 314

> It is something that can not be treated as a small matter that men who have had so much light, and such clear evidence as to the genuineness of the truth we hold, should become unsettled, and led to accept spiritualistic theories regarding the personality of God. [288]

This book suggests that we see much the same today, though it was only a period of six years from Dr. Kellogg's introduction of pantheistic thought at the General Conference of 1897 until it became a major issue in 1903. Our current circumstances have been in the making for a much longer time.

2. The views presented by Dr. Kellogg—both in his book, *The Living Temple*, and in his public and private statements to others—presented God as *in* all created things.

The same is seen today, in the more completely developed elements of the mystical experience. There are, one would suspect, many people who have had some involvement with a range of emergent ideas and practices who may not have experienced this aspect of the movement's teachings. Praise the Lord for that, just as we would praise Him for the sincere individual who has attended a Pentecostal church but never spoke in tongues. But the experiences of these "preserved ones" do not prove that this teaching is not present in the movement. The evidence is too prevalent to doubt, and may be ignored only at great risk.

3. Ellen White repeatedly remarked that the teachings of the Alpha were similar to errors and heresies she had had to meet in the very early years of her ministry. One element she often cited was a tendency toward sensuality and "free-lovism."

This aspect has not, apparently, been present in the current development. For this we may be thankful. God's church would be wise, however, to be watchful in this regard. It is possible that, once again, "the free-love tendencies of these teachings" may be "so concealed" as to be "difficult to present ... in their real character." [289]

---

288 *Special Testimonies* Series B, No. 7, 37

289 See page 42. If one were to grant a larger scope to a present day "free-lovism" than we find reported in the 1840s, it is worth noting that there is a link developing between

4. Proponents of the Alpha teachings repeatedly tried to equate their positions with the teachings of Ellen White.

Some examples of this are present today. Both the Bible and the Spirit of Prophecy have been claimed as support for the emergent views and practices, but there has been more simple neglect of the Spirit of Prophecy than there has been an effort to claim it as an ally. It is difficult to make Ellen White say what she did not mean to say, just because of the volume and clarity of her writings. The only real chance of success in this way is to find where she has said something superficially similar to what one wants to support. [290]

5. The Spirit of Prophecy speaks of Kellogg's teaching as "spiritu-alistic," both in the sense of "spiritualizing away" the truths of the Bible, and also in the sense of involving the direct agency of demonic forces.

It is not easy to point to any particular objective evidence of this in today's circumstances. The similarity between the fully de-veloped contemplative experience and other more clearly demon-ic systems of belief and practice is striking in some cases. If one is willing to accept the testimony of those who have come out of the various forms of Eastern mysticism, these similarities make a strong case, but this apparently is not considered solid evidence in some people's estimation.

Perhaps the most important parallel of Kellogg's day is that there was nothing that could be pointed out as overt evidence of demon-ic involvement. Nothing being thrown across the room, no ghostly apparitions. But Ellen White had no doubt as to the source and the spirit behind the doctor's behavior and theories.

Those who had faith in the Spirit of Prophecy were convinced; those who doubted, doubted. That much hasn't changed.

The five characteristics we have considered here are based on the observed features of the Alpha. But there is another, perhaps even more relevant list of characteristics. When Ellen White wrote the

emergent theology and the gay rights movement. See the footnote on pages 142–143 for one example. Within Adventism, this connection is seen in support for the film Seventh-Gay Adventists, and likely in the call for "racial and gender equality" given prominence by the newly formed Adventist Peace Fellowship. See page 169.

290 See examples of this on pages 116 and 118–119.

famous iceberg vision in 1903, she spoke of the Alpha then current and asked a rhetorical question as to its future:

> The enemy of souls has sought to bring in the supposition that a great reformation was to take place among Seventh-day Adventists, and that this reformation would consist in giving up the doctrines which stand as the pillars of our faith, and engaging in a process of reorganization. Were this reformation to take place, what would result?

Answering her own question, she gave a number of predictions as to what the Alpha would become if allowed to develop unopposed. These predictions should logically apply—at least to a good degree—to anything that deserves consideration as a fulfillment of the Omega prophecy.

> The principles of truth that God in His wisdom has given to the remnant church, would be discarded. Our religion would be changed. The fundamental principles that have sustained the work for the last fifty years would be accounted as error. A new organization would be established. Books of a new order would be written. A system of intellectual philosophy would be introduced. The founders of this system would go into the cities, and do a wonderful work. The Sabbath, of course, would be lightly regarded, as also the God who created it. Nothing would be allowed to stand in the way of the new movement. The leaders would teach that virtue is better than vice, but God being removed, they would place their dependence on human power, which, without God, is worthless. Their foundation would be built on the sand, and storm and tempest would sweep away the structure. [291]

The first several items are quite easily seen in the devlopments that have been discussed in previous chapters, but the specification about a "wonderful work" in the cities is of special interest. Dr. Kellogg's unbalanced city mission work in Chicago and elsewhere was no doubt the primary application of this in 1903. But what of today? Is there any parallel?

---

291 *Selected Messages*, Book One, 204–205

The most recent public development in this arena is the launching of the Adventist Peace Fellowship. This organization, a peer of the "peace fellowships" formed by Buddhists, Baptists, Catholics, Muslims, and other religious groups,[292] claims strong support from many of the same individuals who are prominent within, or supportive of, the One Project. The APF website says the new organization's goals:

- Peacemaking and Reconciliation: We support strategies of nonviolent conflict resolution and ecumenical dialogue.

- Health and Human Rights: We support the right of all persons to care that honors their dignity and worth.

- Caring for Creation: We support environmental stewardship, conservation, and the rights of animals.

- Freedom of Conscience: We support liberty of conscience and free speech for persons of all beliefs or none.

- Racial and Gender Equality: We support the equal human rights of all persons made in the image of God.

- Sabbath Economics: We support debt relief for developing nations and a preferential option for the poor.[293]

To discuss the full scope of each of these priorities is more than space will allow. There is obviously some merit in each of these positions, though the question of boundaries arises in nearly all, with the most obvious theological and moral concerns coming in the areas of ecumenical dialog and gender equality. The novel application of the Sabbath to matters of economics is also worth noting.

Though certainly not exclusively, the Adventist Peace Fellowship is well supported by those sympathetic to the other organizations and causes we have discussed.[294]

---

292 adventistpeace.org/about/frequently-asked-questions

293 adventistpeace.org

294 See adventistpeace.org/about/our-officers-and-board. As one indication of the organization's openness, the advisory board includes former Adventist pastor Ryan Bell, who wrote in the *Huffington Post*: "I will 'try on' atheism for a year. For the next 12 months I will live as if there is no God. I will not pray, read the Bible for inspiration, refer to God as the cause of things or hope that God might intervene and change my own or someone else's circumstances." huffingtonpost.com/ryan-j-bell/a-year-without-god_b_4512842.html

But if Ellen White is to be believed, pantheistic teachings and practices result in "God being removed" from such enterprises. Dr. Kellogg would have vigorously protested such a charge, of course. Certainly the Alpha included much talk of God, but Ellen White points directly to the matter of "dependence on human power,"[295] and concludes that "storm and tempest would sweep away the structure."

We are left with two questions: Do the principles of the emergent movement place it in parallel with those of the Alpha? And, if so, do we trust the warning given by the Spirit of Prophecy?

---

295 Ellen White pointed to this tendency to put "man where God should be" as the root cause of most if not all the problems experienced by the church in her day. For background, see chapters 13, 14, 17, 21, and 39 of *Hindsight: Seventh-day Adventist History in Essays and Extracts.*

Chapter Twenty
Full Circle

W HAT have we learned from all this? We started with the Alpha of Apostasy in the early 1900s. A century and more later, we're looking at a reasonable approximation of the predicted Omega of Apostasy.

For the sake of clarity, let it be understood that this volume makes no claims that these issues definitely do constitute the Omega. Only the Lord Himself knows that for sure. But our circumstances now, and the damage being done to the church, are certainly in the Omega category. There is no reason whatsoever to not raise an alarm. It seems obvious that we've come to a time that is similar to the conditions of Kellogg's day. To some degree, perhaps even more than back then, these thoughts apply:

> The sentiments in *Living Temple* regarding the personality of God have been received even by men who have had a long experience in the truth. When such men consent to eat of the fruit of the tree of knowledge of good and evil, we are no longer to regard the subject as a matter to be treated with the greatest delicacy. That those whom we thought sound in the faith should have failed to discern the specious, deadly influence of this science of evil, should alarm us as nothing else has alarmed us.

> It is something that can not be treated as a small matter that men who have had so much light, and such clear evidence as to the genuineness of the truth we hold, should become unsettled, and led to accept spiritualistic theories regarding the personality of God. [296]

Though we are not judges of thought and motive, the evidence that some among us have "become unsettled" is too much to ignore. The "greatest delicacy" must now be put aside—but not the greatest

---

296 *Special Testimonies* Series B, No. 7, 37

love. As a justified "alarm" spurs God's people to action, there is instruction and assurance which may be found in the account of the Alpha conflict. The story of the climax of the *Living Temple* controversy in 1903 is well known, but still it bears repeating here:

> Shortly before I sent out the testimonies regarding the efforts of the enemy to undermine the foundation of our faith through the dissemination of seductive theories, I had read an incident about a ship in a fog meeting an iceberg. For several nights I slept but little. I seemed to be bowed down as a cart beneath sheaves. One night a scene was clearly presented before me. A vessel was upon the waters, in a heavy fog. Suddenly the lookout cried, "Iceberg just ahead!" There, towering high above the ship, was a gigantic iceberg. An authoritative voice cried out, "Meet it!" There was not a moment's hesitation. It was a time for instant action. The engineer put on full steam, and the man at the wheel steered the ship straight into the iceberg. With a crash she struck the ice. There was a fearful shock, and the iceberg broke into many pieces, falling with a noise like thunder to the deck. The passengers were violently shaken by the force of the collisions, but no lives were lost. The vessel was injured, but not beyond repair. She rebounded from the contact, trembling from stem to stern, like a living creature. Then she moved forward on her way.

> Well I knew the meaning of this representation. I had my orders. I had heard the words, like a voice from our Captain, "Meet it!" I knew what my duty was, and that there was not a moment to lose. The time for decided action had come. I must without delay obey the command, "Meet it!"

> That night I was up at one o'clock, writing as fast as my hand could pass over the paper. For the next few days I worked early and late, preparing for our people the instruction given me regarding the errors that were coming in among us.

> I have been hoping that there would be a thorough reformation, and that the principles for which we fought in the early

days, and which were brought out in the power of the Holy Spirit, would be maintained. [297]

Let us close our review of the past and present with this thought; that the "principles for which we fought in the early days ... would be maintained." In the early 1900s we fought for those principles again, and by God's grace His church won a victory. But history has shown that we grasped only some of the principles in those days. We defended our theology, the heart of our message, but in that battle we lost our right arm ... and hardly noticed. We've been paying for it ever since. [298]

Remember Ellen White's effort to save Kellogg, defending him at the 1903 General Conference ... a full year after *The Living Temple* was written! Remember her work for Dr. Edwards and Dr. Paulson, and her charge to them that if Kellogg were to be lost, it should only be with their hands on his shoulders, trying to save him.

This is not to minimize the seriousness of Kellogg's errors. After a whole book decrying the echoes of his false teachings, let no one think that they were insignificant! They were soul-destroying heresy that threatened to sink God's church. And yet... and yet Dr. Kellogg was also a soul that needed salvation. One of the "principles for which we fought in the early days" was lost sight of in our dealings with Kellogg. And today, we must not repeat the error of ramming the iceberg at less than "full steam," or of failing to aim the ship "straight into the iceberg."[299]

Immediately following the sentence about principles of the early days, Ellen White wrote,

---

297 *Selected Messages*, Book One, 205–206

298 We again recommend *d'Sozo: Reversing the Worst Evil*, available from Remnant Publications, to all who wish to understand the history surrounding Dr. Kellogg and the "worst evil" (Ellen White's term) that has been placed on our churches for the last century and more, partially at least as a result of the manner in which his case was handled.

299 This was the mistake that sealed the fate of the Titanic. The captain, seeking to avoid a collision, ended up side-swiping the iceberg. A head-on impact would have collapsed the bow and badly damaged the ship, but the waterproof hatches would have held the water in only the fore compartments. Instead, the glancing blow popped the rivets all down the side of the ship, flooding more than half the water-tight compartments of the vessel. Once that was done, simple physics made it impossible for her to remain afloat.

Many of our people do not realize how firmly the foundation of our faith has been laid. My husband, Elder Joseph Bates, Father Pierce, Elder Edson, and others who were keen, noble, and true, were among those who, after the passing of the time in 1844, searched for the truth as for hidden treasure.

With nothing more than that as a transition, she abruptly shifts from addressing pantheism and recounts the story of this small study group which met whenever possible as they tried to understand the Lord's leading from the time of the Millerite movement on. One short paragraph brings the focus back to her present time and the attack being made on the core truths of the church. Then she writes this:

I have the tenderest feelings toward Dr. Kellogg. For many years I have tried to hold fast to him. God's word to me has always been, "You can help him." Sometimes I am awakened in the night, and, rising, I walk the room, praying: "O Lord, hold Dr. Kellogg fast. Do not let him go. Keep him steadfast. Anoint his eyes with the heavenly eyesalve, that he may see all things clearly." Night after night I have lain awake, studying how I could help him. Earnestly and often I have prayed that the Lord may not permit him to turn away from sanctifying truth. This is the burden that weighs me down—the desire that he shall be kept from making mistakes that would hurt his soul and injure the cause of present truth. [300]

This may seem strange to us, for Kellogg was the villain in the story, but this, too, was one of the principles of the early days: the determination to understand and hold on to truth—and to do so *together*. This is powerfully spelled out in a parallel passage. Much as we've just read, this passage also starts with that little group of the keen, noble, and true:

My husband, with Elders Joseph Bates, Stephen Pierce, Hiram Edson, and others who were keen, noble, and true, was among those who, after the passing of the time in 1844, searched for the truth as for hidden treasure.

---

300 *Special Testimonies*, Series B, No. 2, 58

We would come together burdened in soul, praying that we might be one in faith and doctrine; for we knew that Christ is not divided. One point at a time was made the subject of investigation. The Scriptures were opened with a sense of awe. Often we fasted, that we might be better fitted to understand the truth. After earnest prayer, if any point was not understood it was discussed, and each one expressed his opinion freely; then we would again bow in prayer, and earnest supplications went up to heaven that God would help us to see eye to eye, that we might be one as Christ and the Father are one. Many tears were shed.

We spent many hours in this way. Sometimes the entire night was spent in solemn investigation of the Scriptures, that we might understand the truth for our time. On some occasions the Spirit of God would come upon me, and difficult portions were made clear through God's appointed way, and then there was perfect harmony. We were all of one mind and one spirit.

We sought most earnestly that the Scriptures should not be wrested to suit any man's opinions. We tried to make our differences as slight as possible by not dwelling on points that were of minor importance, upon which there were varying opinions. But the burden of every soul was to bring about a condition among the brethren which would answer the prayer of Christ that His disciples might be one as He and the Father are one.

Sometimes one or two of the brethren would stubbornly set themselves against the view presented, and would act out the natural feelings of the heart; but when this disposition appeared, we suspended our investigations and adjourned our meeting, that each one might have an opportunity to go to God in prayer and, without conversation with others, study the point of difference, asking light from heaven. With expressions of friendliness we parted, to meet again as soon as possible for further investigation. At times the power of God came upon us in a marked manner, and when clear light revealed the points of truth, we would weep and rejoice together. We loved Jesus; we loved one another.[301]

This is the spirit in which we must ram the iceberg. Only when our ship is equipped with all the armor and weaponry of God can we expect to successfully navigate the waters through which we are called to sail. Without genuine love for God and His truth, combined with genuine love for our neighbors (and, even harder sometimes, our fellow Adventists) our efforts will fall short. We will fall short.

We have been told: "The Omega will follow, and will be received by those who are not willing to heed the warning God has given."[302]

Remember, the challenge is two-fold. Not only must we "contend earnestly for the faith which was once for all delivered to the saints,"[303] but we must also work to answer Christ's prayer "that they all may be one, as You, Father, are in Me, and I in You; that they also may be one in Us, that the world may believe that You sent Me."[304]

This evidence, the unity and love of God's people, must yet be presented to the world—and to the watching universe. In yet another parallel passage, Ellen White tells the story of those who humbled themselves to one another as they studied together. Just after the comment that "We loved Jesus; we loved one another," she continues with these recollections and admonitions:

> In those days God wrought for us, and the truth was precious to our souls. It is necessary that our unity today be of a character that will bear the test of trial. We are in the school of the Master here, that we may be trained for the school above. We must learn to bear disappointment in a Christ-like manner, and the lesson taught by this will be of great importance to us.

> We have many lessons to learn, and many, many to unlearn. God and heaven alone are infallible. Those who think that they will never have to give up a cherished view, never have occasion to change an opinion, will be disappointed. As long as we

---

301 *Testimonies to Ministers*, 25

302 *Selected Messages*, Book One, 200

303 Jude 1:3

304 John 17:21

hold to our own ideas and opinions with determined persisten-
cy, we cannot have the unity for which Christ prayed. [305]

Here is where we are to find the humility, the honesty, the community, the relationship for which many within our church and the
world around us are longing. Here is the experience of fellowship
with Christ and like-minded believers. Here—among those who
have received from Christ the Words of His Father that they might
be sanctified[306]—will be exhibited the glory of God's character. Giv-
en by the Father to Christ, and given by Him to us, this glory is to be
the final evidence to the world. We are to show in our own lives how
all who will acknowledge from the heart that "thy word is truth"[307]
can "be made perfect in one, and that the world may know that You
have sent Me, and have loved them as You have loved Me." [308]

The challenge we face is not only to defend our doctrine, though
surely this must be done. The challenge is to defend it as Jesus defended His mission from Judas, and as Ellen White defended the
truth from John Kellogg, whom she loved as a son.

In His final prayer with and for His disciples, Jesus said to His
Father, "Those whom You gave Me I have kept; and none of them is
lost except the son of perdition."[309] As Ellen White commissioned the
sometimes erring physicians to try and save Dr. Kellogg, Jesus asks
us to seek to save each other. Only in so doing will we find our own
souls preserved.

Strengthened by the prayer we've just been considering, Jesus
walked down the hillside, crossed the Kidron, and staggered into the
horror of great darkness awaiting Him in Gethsemane. There, we are
told, the cup of divine justice trembled in His hands.

More than eighteen hundred years later, the messenger of
the Lord trembled when she saw the Omega of apostasy test
God's church.

Perhaps there is reason enough—both in our own souls and in
our church—that we should tremble, too.

---

305 *Review and Herald*, July 26, 1892

306 John 17:8, 14, 17

307 John 17:17

308 John 17:23

309 John 17:12

Chapter Twenty-one
This Little Light of Mine

CONVENTIONAL wisdom (based on Christ's parable of the lamp and the lampstand, probably) holds that it's better to light a single candle than to curse the darkness. A related Biblical metaphor is the idea of "sighing and crying." There's a place for that; in fact, it seems to be a prerequisite for receiving the seal of God. [310] But even "sighing and crying" will only get God's people so far, and it's never been His plan to use those methods to take "this gospel of the kingdom to all the world."

So what's the point of a book like this? Is it all sighing and crying? Only a matter of defense? Protecting the flock? Largely. But no one has ever won a war with defense alone.

There's a problem, though, with our ideas of offensive warfare. We tend to get confused on one of the most basic points of military doctrine: we don't know who the enemy is. That's quite ridiculous, of course, to go charging off into battle without knowing who we're fighting... but it happens.

So, just for the record, let it be stated again that none of the people or organizations mentioned in this book are the enemy. We don't need to fight people, even should they untiringly advocate error. In fact, a large part of the mission we've been given by our General is to *save* those people... from the real enemy... and, if we should—*God forbid*—fail to save them, let it never be without hands of true friendship on their shoulders.

> We do not wrestle against flesh and blood, but against principalities, against powers, against the rulers of the darkness of this age, against spiritual hosts of wickedness in the heavenly places. [311]

What does the Spirit of Prophecy have to say about fighting the Omega apostasy? Is there anything special that we need to know

---

310 Ezekiel 9:4

311 Ephesians 6:12

about this particular battle? Or is it just the same as all the former battles, only a little more dangerous?

As it turns out, there is one startling aspect of our General's orders for the final battle to which we have paid little attention:

> The truth for this time, the third angel's message, is to be proclaimed with a loud voice, meaning with increasing power, as we approach the great final test. This test must come to the churches in connection with the true medical missionary work, a work that has the great Physician to dictate and preside in all it comprehends. [312]

This test must come to the churches in connection with… *the Sabbath! the state of the dead! the mark of the beast! righteousness by faith!* All true enough, as we know … but that's not what the prophet wrote.

What could "true medical missionary work" ever have to do with the "great final test"?

The answer to this question must, of necessity, be built upon our idea of the nature of the final battle. And that's the second piece of bad news: not only do we tend to get confused as to who the enemy is, we also often fail to understand the battle itself. Simply put (and there is enough for another book in this), we are in a battle of ideas, and the only weapon we have is influence. [313]

> In giving Christ to our world for the redemption of the human family, God planned to change the destructive tendencies of man's influence, and he lays special claim upon that influence, seeks to press it into his service, and by his Holy Spirit sanctify the ability. He wants to make man a chosen vessel unto honor, to be a coworker with him in suppressing evil, and extending righteousness in the earth. Christ, co-operating with human agencies, will restore man to favor with God.

---

312 *Ellen G. White 1888 Materials*, 1710

313 This source veers a little from the main focus of this book, but for understanding the background concepts of this final chapter there is probably no better source than the five-part video series, "Lightning from Heaven," presented by Pastor Kameron DeVasher. Highly recommended. You can find it here: youtube.com/watch?v=-Ur_FjOj6Og&list=PLFoCR8t84rhTY3lWTmheSPKK3jlK8YBn4

Satan planned to draw men's minds away from God, that the knowledge of God might become extinct, and that the human agency might, through his power, become a means of destruction; but Christ, the Restorer, came to counteract the work of Satan, to set in operation plans of the highest order, and by giving man a glimpse of the future world, and the exceeding great reward, to make him see things in their true light. With the golden chain of his matchless love, he would bind men to the throne of God.

The plan of God was that the highest influence in the universe, emanating from the Center of all power, should be brought to bear on human minds. The goodness and love of God subdues the heart, and then man becomes a channel to communicate these divine impressions to his fellow-men. Thus in Christ he is a fruit-bearing branch. No man, saint or sinner, liveth to himself.[314]

These paragraphs are powerful, yet easy to pass over with little thought. We can't afford to do that just now, so let's break it down:

1. Man's influence is evil, but God plans to change it to be a positive element.
2. To do this, God gives "man a glimpse of the future world," emphasizing, not the streets of gold and the mansions, but "the golden chain of His matchless love," aiming to "make him see things in their true light."
3. This "goodness and love of God" is "the highest influence in the universe, emanating from the Center of all power, [and is] brought to bear on human minds."
4. By this means, "man becomes a channel to communicate these divine impressions to his fellow-men."

And another look at influence:

The Lord Jesus has bound up His interests with the interests of the whole world. His influence is an ever-widening, shoreless influence. Although unseen, it is intensely active. Wielded by

---

314 *Signs of the Times*, December 21, 1891

the Father Himself, it is the element which is used in restoring the moral image of God in man.[315]

There it is, *that* influence is the weapon of choice—indeed, the only weapon in the Lord's armory. We cannot generate it; "Wielded by the Father Himself," it comes "from the Center of all power," and once activated in our minds, it transforms us into channels to communicate the same "divine impressions" to others.

But how? How do we pass on this influence to others? The same way Jesus did, of course. That's why we call ourselves "Christ-ians."

Christians, when you took this name, you promised to prepare in this life for the higher life in the kingdom of God. Take the Christlife as your pattern. Keep eternity ever in view. Follow righteous principles of action, which with their refining, ennobling influence will restore in man the moral image of God. As by faith we adopt the principles which are an expression of the life of Christ, they are in the soul as a well of water springing up unto everlasting life. The soul overflows with the riches of the grace of Christ, and the overflow refreshes other souls. Thus may the human agent show that he is keeping the pledge he has made. Thus he may work in partnership with Christ, showing to the world what it means to be a Christian.[316]

"Take the Christlife as your pattern." That certainly sounds like a good idea... but what does it *mean*? What is there about Christ's life that carries the kind of influence we're talking about here?

[Isaiah 58] is the work God requires His people to do. ... With the work of advocating the commandments of God and repairing the breach that has been made in the law of God, we are to mingle compassion for suffering humanity. We are to show supreme love to God; we are to exalt His memorial, which has been trodden down by unholy feet; and with this we are to manifest mercy, benevolence, and the tenderest pity for the fallen race. "Thou shalt love thy neighbor as thyself." As a people

---

315 *Manuscript Releases*, vol. 14, 57

316 *Signs of the Times*, July 10, 1901

we must take hold of this work. Love revealed for suffering humanity gives significance and power to the truth.[317]

Significance... power... *influence?*

Love revealed for suffering humanity... Isaiah 58... mercy, benevolence, and the tenderest pity. ... This is starting to sound like medical missionary work! Indeed, it is; and it's what we need to be doing. *Really?* How? How much? Why?

> Nothing will help us more at this stage of our work than to understand and to fulfill the mission of the greatest Medical Missionary that ever trod the earth; nothing will help us more than to realize how sacred is this kind of work and how perfectly it corresponds with the lifework of the Great Missionary. The object of our mission is the same as the object of Christ's mission. Why did God send His Son to the fallen world? To make known and to demonstrate to mankind His love for them. ...

> God's purpose in committing to men and women the mission that He committed to Christ is to disentangle His followers from all worldly policy and to give them a work identical with the work that Christ did.[318]

Again, let's break this one down:

1. "Nothing will help us more" than to get up to speed on medical missionary work,

2. because "the object of our mission is the same as the object of Christ's mission,"

3. and that is to "demonstrate to mankind [God's] love for them."

4. God's plan is for us to carry on "a work identical with the work that Christ did,"

5. But that requires Him to "disentangle His followers from all worldly policy."

Identical? That's a strong word! Just let that soak in for a while. And what is this "worldly policy" issue? Well, we know that the

317 *Welfare Ministry*, 32

318 *Medical Ministry*, 24

classic policy that people will need to be disentangled from at the end of time will be Sunday worship... but that seems rather far removed from medical missionary work. Until you read this:

> We cannot keep [the Sabbath] holy unless we serve the Lord in the manner brought to view in the scripture: "Is not this the fast that I have chosen, to loose the bands of wickedness, to undo the heavy burdens, and to let the oppressed go free, and that ye break every yoke? Is it not to deal thy bread to the hungry, and that thou bring the poor that are cast out to thy house? when thou seest the naked, that thou cover him; and that thou hide not thyself from thine own flesh?" This is the work that rests upon every soul who accepts the service of Christ.[319]

But how does this all fit together? What's the common denominator in all these ideas? Simply put, it's just faith and love. And if you're wondering how that works, read this:

> All His gifts are to be used in blessing humanity, in relieving the suffering and the needy. We are to feed the hungry, to clothe the naked, to care for the widow and the fatherless, to minister to the distressed and downtrodden. God never meant that the widespread misery in the world should exist. He never meant that one man should have an abundance of the luxuries of life, while the children of others should cry for bread. The means over and above the actual necessities of life are entrusted to man to do good, to bless humanity.
>
> The Lord says, "Sell that ye have, and give alms." Be "ready to distribute, willing to communicate." "When thou makest a feast, call the poor, the maimed, the lame, the blind." "Loose the bands of wickedness," "undo the heavy burdens," "let the oppressed go free," "break every yoke." "Deal thy bread to the hungry," "bring the poor that are cast out to thy house." "When thou seest the naked,... cover him." "Satisfy the afflicted soul." "Go ye into all the world, and preach the gospel to every creature." These are the Lord's commands.[320]

319 *Manuscript Releases*, vol. 5, 33

320 *Christ's Object Lessons*, 370

It's right about here that our faith and love tend to start going squishy on all this. And for a pretty good reason: doing this sort of thing is certainly going to take a lot of time, and likely a fair amount of money, as well. And we're busy people. And we've only got a limited amount of cash. It all certainly seems like a good idea, but we need to be realistic, too.

But what if that kind of thinking turns out to be a "worldly policy"? What if true faith is supposed to say, "Do it anyway"?

Is it unrealistic to look at the daily schedule and personal finances of Christ, and say, "That's good enough for me; I don't need to be any better off than He was"? After all, we *were* told that "A disciple is not above his teacher, nor a servant above his master. It is enough for a disciple that he be like his teacher, and a servant like his master."[321] And again: "A disciple is not above his teacher, but everyone who is perfectly trained will be like his teacher."[322]

Is that part of "a work identical with the work that Christ did"?

Really, what are "the actual necessities of life"?

And what percentage of the "means over and above" those necessities is supposed to go to helping others?

Sadly, it's safe to say that there are probably far more—and often far better—examples of this kind of activity among the sincere-at-heart members of the "fallen churches" than among Seventh-day Adventists, especially among some of the emergent folks. In this matter of service to others, they have stolen (half) a march on us. What are they missing? Look for it:

> Get the young men and women in the churches to work. Combine medical missionary work with the proclamation of the third angel's message. Make regular, organized efforts to lift the church members out of the dead level in which they have been for years. Send out into the churches workers who will live the principles of health reform. Let those be sent who can see the necessity of self-denial in appetite, or they will be a snare to the church. See if the breath of life will not then come into our churches. A new element needs to be brought into the work.[323]

321 Matthew 10:24–25

322 Luke 6:40

323 *Testimonies*, vol. 6, 267

Did you spot it? The social responsibility common in the emergent movement isn't all bad… but it needs to be combined with the third angel's message! Not some mystical influence that contradicts the Bible.

And, did you notice the result that is promised if this work is carried out? "See if the breath of life will not then come into our churches." This is probably the most basic concern that the emergent movement has tried to address: *"Religion is boring! The church members are dead! We need to do something new!"*

They aren't all wrong… at least not if you believe Ellen White's assessment. But if you believe Ellen White's assessment, you'll be combining "medical missionary work… with the proclamation of the third angel's message," not *lectio divina*, labyrinths, guided meditation, breath prayers, rock music, and NFL game day barbecues!

We were given the answer to our challenges a century ago. The diagnosis is similar, but the prescription is vastly different. And there's only one problem… that whole thing about it taking up so much of our time and money.

"That's really inconvenient… and impractical… unrealistic… the sort of thing that might have worked a century ago, in a simpler time, when everybody just lived on a farm and had nothing going on anyway. But not today! Life is soooo busy! And the bills! They just keep coming every month. What am I supposed to do about them?"

> He who has pity on the poor lends to the Lord, and He [big "H"] will pay back what he [little "h"] has given.[324]

How much faith do we have in that promise? How much faith do we have in any of His promises?

> We shall not be stinted for means if we will only go forward trusting in God. The Lord is willing to do a great work for all who truly believe in Him. If the lay members of the church will arouse to do the work that they can do, going on a warfare at their own charges, each seeing how much he can accomplish in winning souls to Jesus, we shall see many leaving the ranks of Satan to stand under the banner of Christ. If our people will act upon the light that is given in these few words of instruction,

---

324 Proverbs 19:17

we shall surely see of the salvation of God. Wonderful revivals will follow. Sinners will be converted, and many souls will be added to the church. When we bring our hearts into unity with Christ, and our lives into harmony with His work, the Spirit that fell on the disciples on the Day of Pentecost will fall on us. [325]

How much love do we have for other people? Not just our friends, but all those other folks, as well?

The problem our church faces today is too much stuff, and too little faith and love. Or did you really believe the story that "rich and increased with goods" had nothing to do with being "rich and increased with goods"? All those riches, all those goods, "over and above the actual necessities of life are entrusted to man to do good, to bless humanity."

And the lack of faith and love? We had someone tell us about that, once upon a time.

The gold mentioned by Christ, the True Witness, which all must have, has been shown me to be faith and love combined. … Satan is constantly at work to remove these precious gifts from the hearts of God's people. [326]

"Behold, I stand at the door, and knock: if any man hear my voice, and open the door, I will come in to him, and will sup with him, and he with me." The position of Christ is the attitude of forbearance and importunity. "I counsel thee to buy of me gold tried in the fire, that thou mayest be rich." O, the soul-poverty is alarming! And those who are most in need of the gold of love, feel rich and increased with goods, when they lack every grace. Having lost faith and love, they have lost everything. [327]

"But, seriously, what can we do? We're losing our young people right and left. They don't feel like they're a part of anything important, and the routine church service just doesn't have the kind of impact on their personal lives they are looking for. Some of them have an interest in evangelism, but how many of our youth can we realistically expect

---

325 *Testimonies*, vol. 8, 246

326 *Testimonies*, vol. 2, 36

327 *Review and Herald*, December 23, 1890

to see up on public stage doing that sort of thing? Besides, there is a diminishing rate of return on the whole evangelistic series approach. It's all kind of discouraging."

Of course it's discouraging! We haven't been following the only instructions that will succeed!

> Unless there are those who will devise means of turning to account the time, strength, and brains of the church members, there will be a great work left undone that ought to be done. Haphazard work will not answer. We want men in the church who have ability to develop in the line of organizing and giving practical work to young men and women in the line of relieving the wants of humanity, and working for the salvation of the souls of men, women, youth, and children.[328]

> Because so little effort has been made to engage young men and women in the missionary work which must be done to bring the gospel invitation to all, there is but one worker where there should be a hundred. The indifference which is manifested for suffering humanity is charged against churches and families and individuals. … Churches that ought to work in Christ's lines are inclined to make disparaging remarks of those who engage in medical missionary work. And yet they profess to be the people of God.

> True Christlike compassion will be manifested in seeking to save those who are lost, looking for them not only in the churches, but also in the world. The woes of men are to be met by all who believe in Christ: the lost are to be sought for on every side; restoration is to be begun. Compassion manifested for the physical necessities opens the way for the soul to be reached.[329]

> The work that the Great Teacher did in connection with His disciples is the example we are to follow. …

---

328 *Welfare Ministry*, 105

329 *Review and Herald*, March 1, 1898

It is only by an unselfish interest in those in need of help that we can give a practical demonstration of the truths of the gospel. ...

The Lord will give you success in this work; for the gospel is the power of God unto salvation when it is interwoven with the practical life, when it is lived and practiced. The union of Christlike work for the body and Christlike work for the soul is the true interpretation of the gospel.[330]

Did you catch that? "*The* true interpretation." Not "*a* true interpretation." Not "the interpretation of the Christians" as compared to some "equally valid interpretation of the Hindus," or the Sufis, or the Buddhists, or the Taoists, or the Catholics, or the Jesuits, or the Charismatics, or... anyone. Medical missionary work is the way Jesus worked. And it's the only way we'll ever have real success.

Christ's method alone will give true success in reaching the people. The Saviour mingled with men as one who desired their good. He showed His sympathy for them, ministered to their needs, and won their confidence. Then He bade them, "Follow Me."[331]

But more than success in reaching the people, it's only by putting ourselves out into the realm of *this-isn't-going-to-work-without-God's-help* that we begin to grow, ourselves.[332] Do you want some real meaning in your Christian life? Stick your neck out a bit.[333]

---

330 *Review and Herald*, March 4, 1902

331 *Ministry of Healing*, 143

332 Here's a little mental exercise to try: Think through all the really good Bible stories, the ones you could use as a bedtime story for a seven-year-old. How many of them don't feature someone who would have been in a world of hurt if God hadn't gotten involved in the story? Do you really think those stories are there just for the seven-year-olds?

333 Do it honestly, though, because there aren't any promises that apply to pretentious hypocrites. Remember, you can't pick and choose among Jesus' instructions. You may not be "perfect," but you need to not be rebellious. That's the difference between faith and presumption.

Every one needs a practical experience in trusting God for himself. Let no man become your confessor;[334] open the heart to God; tell Him every secret of the soul. Bring to Him your difficulties, small and great, and He will show you a way out of them all. He alone can know how to give the very help you need.

And when, after a trying season, help comes to you, when the Spirit of God is manifestly at work for you, what a precious experience you gain! You are obtaining faith and love, the gold that the True Witness counsels you to buy of Him. You are learning to go to God in all your troubles; and as you learn these precious lessons of faith, you will teach the same to others. Thus you may be continually leading the people to a higher plane of experience.[335]

Oh—that thing about evangelism not being so successful—this is the answer for that, too.

Search heaven and earth, and there is no truth revealed more powerful than that which is made manifest in works of mercy to those who need our sympathy and aid. This is the truth as it is in Jesus. When those who profess the name of Christ shall practice the principles of the golden rule, the same power will attend the gospel as in apostolic times.[336]

In no way could the Lord be better glorified and the truth more highly honored than for unbelievers to see that the truth has wrought a great and good work upon the lives of naturally covetous and penurious men. If it could be seen that the faith of such had an influence to mold their characters, to change them from close, selfish, overreaching, money-loving men to men who love to do good, who seek opportunities to use their means to bless those who need to be blessed, who visit the widow and fatherless

---

334 "Let no man become your confessor" may appear to be a simple comment made in passing, but it has a real bearing on the whole concept of the work undertaken by "spiritual directors."

335 *Gospel Workers*, 419

336 *Mount of Blessing*, 137

in their affliction, and who keep themselves unspotted from the world, it would be an evidence that their religion was genuine.[337]

"No truth revealed more powerful. ..."
"In no way could the Lord be better glorified. ..."
Doing good... like Jesus. It's a fairly simple, idea, really. Once upon a time, Jesus called it the second commandment, and said "You shall love your neighbor as yourself."[338] But He also gave us the first commandment, and it starts off with "Hear, O Israel, the Lord our God, the Lord is one."

Here is a spiritual unity we can believe in. The kind of unity Jesus prayed for just before the crucifixion:

> This is eternal life, that they may know You, the only true God, and Jesus Christ whom You have sent. ...
>
> For I have given to them the words which You have given Me; and they have received them. ...
>
> Sanctify them by Your truth. Your word is truth. ...
>
> That they all may be one, as You, Father, are in Me, and I in You; that they also may be one in Us, that the world may believe that You sent Me. And the glory [character] which You gave Me I have given them, that they may be one just as We are one. [339]

Here is a field in which the idealism of the One Project could light a constructive fire in God's church! Trembling is proper, sometimes. But it's time to move past the trembling. It's time to start shaking things up a bit. Change *is* needed, but following God's directions will actually work; writing our own script is a disaster.

---

337 *Testimonies*, vol. 2, 239

338 Mark 22:39

339 John 17:3, 8, 17, 21–22

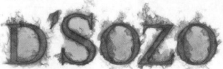

D'SOZO

Reversing the worst evil

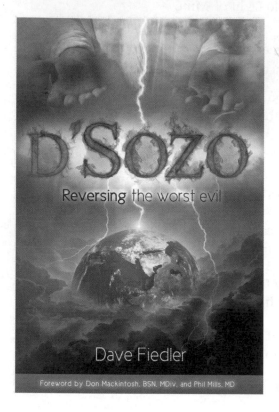

by Dave Fiedler

Dave Fiedler spent twenty years in Adventist classrooms sharing his love for common sense and history with scholars from fifth grade through college. In 2008, the Lord provided opportunity to finally move beyond theory and establish Adventist City Missions.

$19.99
ISBN: 978-1-62407-952-8
AC1002

---

d'Sozo comes from the Greek root which the New Testament uses for both spiritual salvation and physical healing.

But as the Lord's weapon to reverse the worst evil, d'Sozo grows to become an unshakable confidence in God's provision for every need, which frees His people to practice Jesus' combined ministry to body, mind, and soul; makes manifest the divine glory of self-renouncing love; refutes the devil's assertion that self-interest is best; and proves that sinners can, through faith in Christ, become obedient to the "law of life" and safe for re-introduction to the universe of the unfallen.

History, inspiration, and prophecy combine to paint a picture of the end like you've never seen before. God's plan is do-able, and you can be part of it!